SECOND ACTS *that* CHANGE LIVES

SECOND ACTS *that* CHANGE LIVES

Mary Beth Sammons

Making a *Difference* in the World

Conari Press

To my father, Paul Von Driska, who taught me to never, ever give up hope. Through his living he gave testimony to where there is a will, there is a way, and proved that there always is a second chance.

First published in 2009 by
Red Wheel/Weiser, LLC
With offices at:
500 Third Street, Suite 230
San Francisco, CA 94107
www.redwheelweiser.com

ISBN: 978-1-57324-368-1
Library of Congress Cataloging-in-Publication Data
Sammons, Mary Beth.
Second acts that change lives : making a difference in the world / Mary
Beth Sammons.
p. cm.
ISBN 978-1-57324-368-1 (alk. paper)
1. Career changes. 2. Self-actualization (Psychology) I. Title.
HF5384.S25 2009
650.14 — dc22
20080

Cover design by Jessica Dacher
Text design by Jessica Dacher
Typeset in Bembo, Placebo, and Helvetica Neue

Printing in Canada
TCP
10 9 8 7 6 5 4 3 2 1

Contents

Don't be afraid your life will end;
be afraid it will never begin.

— GRACE HANSON

chapter 1

Wake Up! Life's Half Over!
What do I need to do to make a difference?

Have you forgotten to ask yourself the one big question: *What should I do with my life?* For most people, it's a very difficult one to answer. But, now, here you are, at midlife, and suddenly you realize that you have never fully answered this question. You're not living the life of your dreams. In fact, you are desperately seeking inspiration to pursue your dreams and the impact you are meant to have on the world!

All of a sudden, you realize that you have spent the first half of your life concentrating on what you *do,* instead of focusing on what kind of person you *want* to be, what kind of person you *can* be, and how the kind of person you are will change the world, or at least will make a difference in your own life and the lives of others.

Here are some clues that it is time to make a change. Does the thought of spending the next twenty years living the way you are now make you want to crawl back under the covers? Maybe your life is stable, secure, relatively successful, but when people ask you how you are doing, you answer, "I'm not unhappy." Hearing yourself, you discover that not unhappy is becoming increasingly unacceptable.

Or, maybe you've come to the point where your children are getting more independent, and you realize that having them and raising them to this point was an athletic endeavor in itself. At forty-five, you have lost touch with your inner jock. After all the years of being a patient, giving parent, it's time to hop on a bicycle, be aggressive, and get your *grrr* back.

Is there something you've always wanted to do but never dreamed it was possible? Compete in an Ironman? Open a bakery? Write a book? Surf? Climb mountains? Volunteer at an animal rescue shelter? Launch a foundation? Be a hospice volunteer?

Do friends tell you, "Wow, you're really funny; you should be a stand-up comic," or "You're awesome at fundraising"? But, you've never fully come to realize what those skills could mean — to yourself and to the world. Maybe it's time to think like an elite athlete, or at least start testing yourself in a singles tennis league. Or a hang a shingle over your door and start baking pies for business. Take a comedy writing class at Second City. Bake a tray of lasagna for the local soup kitchen. Raise your hand to plan the 5K fund-raiser for your local cancer society.

Are you starting to question, *What's it all about?* Your 9-to-5 is stale, seems meaningless in the larger scheme of things, and you don't want to keel over at your desk one day and call it a life. Do you find yourself pondering the deeper questions: *What do I really want out of my life?* Maybe your heart just isn't in your work. It takes passion and courage to find a profession that you love. You've been so busy racking up titles, hours, and paychecks that you've never had the chance to spend the time to discover what you could do that would make a difference in your life.

Maybe you walk around every day wondering how your life is making a difference in the lives of others, in the world. You want to find a way to take your passions and give back, not just get a paycheck and engrave an impressive job title on your tombstone.

Are you finding yourself increasingly obsessed with dreams of *Oh, someday I'd love to . . . ?* It's time to shed the same old, same old.

Somewhere out there is the thing you were born for, and it's not too late. *Second Acts That Change Lives: Making a Difference in the World* is here to help you get started. The good news: The power to transform your life is much closer than you realize. In these pages, I've brought together a community of people — women and men — who are proving that it's never too late to take a life leap, whether it's starting a new business, leaving the corporate scene to teach high school, turning that great idea into a novel, rock climbing, or adopting a child at fifty-two. The stories are a little bold, a little edgy, and meant to inspire us to tap into the power inside . . . so that we can inspire others, including our children, to tap into their energy and power as well.

In this book, you will meet some brave people who traded successful, safe career paths for the chance to find their true purpose in life. In finding themselves, they were able to find the parts of themselves that can make the world a better place.

Are you looking for your calling, and not just another career? If you are, you know it. You feel it. Your heart is tugging at you to make a difference, to find the place in you where your passions lie; the place in you that really matters, that can make a difference.

Now, it's time to make your next move. There will always be sound reasons and collective voices convincing you to freeze in your tracks: your teachers told you (they told Jane Austen the same thing) that you can't make a living with your pen. How many people have cautioned you, "You've got two kids in college"; "The timing isn't right"; and a million other reasons not to step out now? Family, friends, the local barista, your own inner critic, are all too happy to supply the *con* lists.

"At your age?"

"You're having a midlife crisis."

"What about health insurance?"

"Well, good luck, but I know I couldn't run even a mile at 'our' age. You know, there's a water aerobics class."

"When do you have time to write a book?"

"Just give it up; menopause is going to make you fat. There's nothing you can do."

I know all about this. I've heard them all. I've learned to smile, nod, and realize people mean well. But, I recognize I've spent fifty-plus years on this planet listening to all the "You can'ts," "I can'ts," "You shoulds," "You shouldn'ts."

I'm the master of hanging back, often because I was too embarrassed to be out there, acting like a determined athlete, pursuing career goals and passions, or making time to squeeze my own life into my daily routine. I feel lucky to have discovered some new and some renewed passions halfway through life. This book is meant to prompt you, as author Grace Paley says, "Hey you, begin again? Again, again, you'll see it's easy, begin again."

Second Acts That Change Lives: Making a Difference in the World is a collection of honest and inspiring stories that delve into the lives of a community of trailblazers — second act reinventors — who have paid attention to the stirrings to change, pondered their next move, and turned their "Oh, someday I'd love to" dreams into an adventure, an adventure that is making a profound difference in the world. What I have learned, and these stories underscore, is that, when you ask yourself, *So how do I know where to go?* the answer is, "Follow your heart." Risk and reward are a package. But, you have to make the first move. And when you do, you will be surprised at how the universe moves to guide you. You will be surprised at how wanting more out of life opens the door for you to give more to life. When we surface the best parts of ourselves, somehow we make the world brighter too.

It's not easy. This book is a wake-up call, an intervention of sorts to help prod you. The thread that weaves all of these stories together is the inspiration provided by others who have done it — now you can too!

Meet Marianne, 56, a librarian from Detroit, who lost her husband and soul mate and discovered solace in the unexpected. At age fifty-two, she went to an orphanage in Siberia to meet two children, brother and sister, ages three and five. She brought them home, learned Russian, and today is a single mom of two tweens. See what's gotten into Mary, who at forty-five took a volunteer job with at-risk teenagers and two years later created a pilot curriculum for them, left her six-figure income, conventional marketing career path, and committed herself to these teens as her life's work. Read about Bob, who at sixty-five rode his bike across the country to raise money for ALS, cancer, and hospice, all because he read *Tuesdays with Morrie* and realized he needed to make a mark with his life.

The personal stories in this book are affecting, thought provoking, and inspirational. They're a powerful resource for anyone who's really grappling with life direction issues and wants to make a difference with the second half of their lives. For readers who have realized that the time has come to put their great idea into action, but are asking, *But now what?* the book outlines a process for moving from concept to reality. We look to the individuals featured in the stories for inspiration in starting over and identifying the myths and action steps for deciding and putting into place the next moves.

The stories are meant to inspire, to prompt you to realize that it's never too late to create your second act and become a reinventor, no matter how many "I can'ts" you've told yourself. You can kick butt at any age, and in the process restore hope in yourself and those around you. When we reach inside ourselves to discover who we really are and what we are meant to do, we walk back into the world a little taller, smiling a little more, and experiencing life in ways we never imagined possible. My hope is that you will discover your second act, connect with your passion, and get out there and go after life with all you've got. Can you imagine what will happen as you grab at life, seize the possibilities, and make them yours? It's coming. Watch out world!

Mary Beth's Story

The future belongs to those who believe in the beauty of their dreams.
— Eleanor Roosevelt

"Wake up. Life's half over."

Those are the words, delivered in a passionate coaching-military drill sergeant way each Friday morning at 6 a.m. by my spin teacher Andrew.

For the past year, I have plunged into this whole exercise/fitness/wellness lifestyle. Why? Because as I approached fifty, I realized I was carrying many things: sadness from a shattered marriage; the sudden loss of two close friends and my cousin, just a year younger than me; the stress of trying to raise three teens on my own; and the frightening possibility that I would be just that — alone — forever.

I was scared and confused and didn't know where to turn. So, I decided that what I could do was get out of bed every day and haul myself to a gym. I hoped that maybe by pumping some life into the fibromyalgia syndrome TV commercials insisted was right around the corner, I could refocus my energy and reclaim my old self. I wanted to revitalize the verve lost in the trampling of many dreams. I didn't know what else to do. I had forgotten what my dreams even were.

As slowly as my life had spun itself out of control, I was beginning to develop a new cadence on a stationary spin bicycle. Andrew's orders — "Wake up, life's half over" — became my catalyst. I paid serious attention to his words. I wasn't so much getting into the exercise groove and sweating profusely just to make my legs spin faster and harder on the bike, but to make sure that every day I am alive, I am living, striving faster and harder. The more I sweat, the faster my heart rate registered, the more I knew I was getting in touch with all I had lost.

Those words — "Wake up, life's half over" — kept taking on a deeper and deeper meaning. I was stepping outside of my comfort zone, and there was no better time than the present — turning fifty — to try to accomplish some things in my life I never imagined possible.

From my friends' and my cousin's shortened lives, I was learning that despite everything, their spirits live on in my life and the lives of my children. In honor of them, I was trying to put determination and guts into every day of my own living.

Competing in a triathlon — swimming, bicycling, and running in one event — became my fiftieth birthday goal.

To some it may seem trivial, but running in a triathlon, then months later in my first half-marathon, became my way of pushing myself to show that as a human being I could exceed far beyond what others — or I myself — thought was possible. Swimming in the event — which *terrified* me — was symbolic of all of demons that had me breaking out in cold sweats in the middle of the night: The fact that my job security was suddenly in question following the sale of the company I worked for and the idea of reentering the dating arena after a twenty-five year hiatus proved to me that I needed to find a new direction that would help me do something to help others make a difference. I am learning to embrace going it alone surrounded by a community of friends and family I am blessed to have.

In addition to lighting my fire with the "wake up" warning, Andrew, who pulled me aside after class the day before the big event, said something I will not forget. "You can do it, in memory of those who can't. . . . You can honor their spirit and their courage to keep living to the very end."

So, that is what I did. I dove into the water, pedaled, and ran my heart across the finish line. My friends' spirits and divine energy carried me.

These days, I've lost a lot of titles — wife, "young" mom, vice president of a company. But I wear a couple new ones: triathlete, half-marathoner, and career and personal life adventurer. I'm trying all kinds of things: I've swung on a trapeze; taken up beach volleyball, traveling, knitting lessons (I'm cranking out scarves like crazy), running my own business, yoga, going to weddings alone, gardening, surfing; and I have an endless list of "to-explores." And, I'm going back to graduate school to get a degree in spiritual direction. I have spent a lifetime gathering people's stories; now I want to help them make meaning out of them.

The athletic front gave me my first push, because it is brand-new. Until this year I had an athletic résumé that looked something like this: "Cheerleader, Junior High School (freckles, smile, and energy as driving forces); Volleyball team, eighth grade; and Pandas swim team (small Catholic school, every one made every team)." Until last year, I had never run a mile. I swam two laps and was breathless. I liked to cycle, but that was with a Burley, going a 5-miles-per-hour pace and stopping every half-mile to serve up a Sippy Cup to one of my kids.

I walked a mean double stroller and occasionally swam at the YMCA . . . as many laps as I could (breaststroke so as not to get my hair wet) before the volunteers raced into the pool to tell me one of my kids was crying hysterically in the nursery and it was time for this aspiring get-the-baby-fat-off mom-athlete to pack her bag and go home. On the day of the triathlon, just two weeks after my fiftieth birthday, I crossed the finish line knowing it was a day of triumph.

The day really was about facing fears of illness, grief, and carrying on when I wanted to give up out of exhaustion, stress, and the uncertainty of what lies ahead. The finish line for all of us is never clearly in sight, but we keep pushing to get there, up the steep hills and through the murky waters. You know you can't give up. And you don't.

A few days before the event, I found a card. It was a picture of a swimmer — bathing cap and all — about to dive in.

Be not the slave of your own past — plunge into the sublime seas, dive deep and swim far, so you shall come back with self-respect with new power. With an advanced experience, that shall explain and over- look the old.

Crossing the finish line, I stopped a moment to give thanks to my friends who had died, Vince, Cara, and my cousin Patrick; to my friends and my children who came to the event to cheer us on; to the ones who got me in the race. I learned that even out of the deepest losses . . . you can get into the race again. You can cross a new finish line . . . but you can never do it alone.

One of my favorite books as a teen was *Brian Piccolo: A Short Season,* about the Chicago Bears football player who faced cancer with such courage. I gave it to my son, Thomas, because I want him to find heroes in life like Brian Piccolo, who show courage every single day.

I take the swimmer card with me now each day, along with the memory of my two friends and my cousin. My hope is that overcoming my own fears is a way to honor the gift they have given me — the appreciation of every minute of living. And, I hold on to these words from Brian Piccolo in all my struggles: "You can't quit. It's a league rule."

We all have the power to change our worlds, and the power to help others do that. The triathlon was just the be- ginning for me. I'm now exploring all kinds of opportunities to use my gifts and talents to make the world a better place, to let go of a 9-to-5 job that keeps me from doing so, to ven- ture into the unknown. I can't wait to explore, to grab on to what lies ahead.

This book is meant to be a message of hope, an inspiration, for all of you (and for me too) who feel stuck. I love these stories, because as a mom, I want my daughters, Caitlin and Emily, and my son, Thomas, to live and breathe in the belief of their own power.

One thing I've learned through my own experience is that it is entirely your own call what you can do. In collecting the stories for this book, I've been privileged to talk to many women and men who are reinventing themselves into bigger and better jobs or becoming globe-trotting volunteers. Some are kicking back from high-powered careers to pursue their passion for painting or landscaping, others are newly minted marathoners or yoga instructors. Most have somehow, through their second acts, found a way to inject meaning and purpose into their own lives and the impact they have on others, whether it is orchestrating a mega-fund-raiser for children's cancer or demonstrating that an out-of-shape, approaching-fifty guy who smokes can cross the finish line of a marathon if he sets his mind and body to the task. What also strikes me is how happy they all are with the choices they have made to step out of their comfort zones and go after their dreams.

But, don't suppose for one minute it was easy. I signed up for a swimming workshop so that I could return to my friends and proclaim, "Oh, well . . . I wanted to, but this swim instructor told me I am not a good enough swimmer to do a triathlon. Done." Instead, he told me to "Shut up and get in the water. We're all afraid." I was busted.

And that's the true meaning of this whole book. We all need someone to push us into the water, when we're afraid to put our heads under, even if the "water" is a new career, a new relationship, leaving an unhealthy one, signing up for an exercise class, or volunteering our time to make a huge difference in someone else's life. We're all terrified to leave the comfortable. None of us is especially confident in our own creativity, and most of us care too much what others think of us and their opinions of how and who we should be.

The great thing about midlife is that somehow, suddenly, this default position of doing for everyone else has shifted to "Stand back, this is *my* time." Or at least there are glimmers of moments throughout the day when you can seize control and make it about you.

Now is your time. Join me and all of the second act reinventors in these pages as we revel in a freedom most of us never expected to have in midlife. By reading about other's feats and firsts, my hope is it will prompt you to stretch yourself beyond your own safety net and open yourself to new possibilities. I'm looking forward to them, and who knows, I may meet some of you climbing a mountain some day. I thank Andrew, my spin instructor, for challenging me to "Wake up, life's half over." How about you? What first do you need to make happen, not someday, but today?

I don't know where my triathlon and running adventures will lead me. I do know they have pointed me in many directions toward roads less traveled. Recently, I quit my full-time job and am reimagining my career at fifty. I've always dreamed big. When I was six and learned to read, I announced I was going to grow up to be a book writer. It took me twenty years paying my overhead and dues as a journalist to land my first book on the shelves of a major bookstore. I wanted to be a mom . . . and I have three beautiful children who are the wellspring of my living.

Yes, a lot of the things I had envisioned are no longer, but I refuse to go into middle age without a fight, without new dreams.

I am grateful to the people in this book who shared their yearnings, disappointments, and fears and are turning the deep questions into powerful calls to action. Please join me as I follow the path of their courage in reinventing what lies ahead.

Here are their stories and some of the lessons I wish I had known before I plunged into the water, unplugged from my corporate title, and swam toward a new shore. Let them cheer you on too, and be gift and guide.

chapter 2

But Now What?
One day you discover something is missing in your life — like a life.

Let the world know you as you are, not as you think
you should be because sooner or later, if you are pos-
ing, you will forget the pose, and then where are you?
— *Fanny Brice*

We often hear of people who, when suddenly confronted by
a wake-up call — a divorce, a company downsizing, a devastating illness, or the unexpected death of a friend or loved
one — vow from here on to change their priorities and how
they live. Wake-up calls are those moments when in the
blink of an eye, life's direction changes suddenly.

Midlife in itself can be a wake-up call. It's typically a
time of profound psychological change that usually occurs
between the ages of forty and fifty-five and often results in
dramatic life changes. The defining symptom is a sense that

the beliefs that have guided you up until now no longer hold meaning. Your life seems boring and dull, and there seems to be a void. You may feel like you can't do anything to change it, to get unstuck.

Suddenly you find yourself asking, *Who am I really? What were my dreams? If I'm not fulfilling my dreams, when will I? What would I do differently if confronted with a wake-up call? Would I travel more? Work more?* Or, you think, *But I don't have any energy to change. I'm exhausted. I've worked so hard, for so long, and this is all I get?*

All the obvious questions and anxieties start waking us up in the middle of the night, begging for answers, and they tap into every ounce of our beings, including the spiritual, emotional, and psychological dimensions of our lives. Midlife is a profoundly significant time in our lives.

We find ourselves asking, *How do I find my inner voice? How do I reclaim my long-neglected passions?* Now is the time to discover our authentic selves and to examine our roles beyond parent, significant other (or not), and career person.

In this chapter, we are inspired by several people who are taking on this rite of passage with spirit and passion. Certainly, they've received wake-up calls, but they have chosen to use them as a starting point, a springboard for transformation. They are using their wake-up calls to change direction and embark on lives lead from their hearts.

If you're stuck in a rut and have decided you can't do anything about it, or at least that is what it seems like, I hope you will be inspired by these stories. The first step in getting on with your life is listening for your own wake-up call and then creating a second act. You need to know when to fold the old one into the new, what to let go of, and what to hold on to in order to move on.

One important thing the stories in this chapter remind us is that reaching for the goal doesn't always mean knowing what path to take. As you will see, it is more about putting your dreams out there and then staying open to the possibilities.

In interviewing all of these second act reinventors, I learned that they all share the following belief and hope, quoted from Rainer Maria Rilke. My wish is you can too:

And now, let us begin the New Year full of all things that have never been.

Engaging the Soul in Purposeful Acts of Kindness

From one of America's most feted music industry giants to hospice director, this woman is digging getting paid to be kind.

I am here while you freak out, or grieve, or laugh, or suffer, or sing. It is a ministry of presence. It is showing up with a loving heart. And it is really, really cool.
— *Kate Braestrup*

Nadine Condon spent a glamorous career in the record industry, building big name celebrities to the top of the record charts. The perks were many:

backstage tickets, limos, first-class trips to four-star resorts across the globe. . . . But then the wake-up call: two of the people closest to her died suddenly. Almost overnight, her focus shifted. What she would discover is what she never imagined: that she would find the most powerful triumphs of the human spirit in those who were the most frail, those facing their final moments of life.

Nadine Condon, 56, Phoenix, Arizona

Act I: Twenty-five-year music business veteran; called the "Godmother of Rock" in the San Francisco Bay Area.

Act II: Professional hospice worker and director of Mission Hospice of San Mateo County until 2007. Later that year she launched a new patient advocate program for Hospice of the Valley, Phoenix, Arizona.

Act III: In the works. "My dream is to write and teach," says Nadine.

New Script

Nadine says she discovered life in the powerful experience of a couple she was called on to help through her job as a hospice volunteer. The wife was in her final stages of dementia, and the husband was struggling with his own formidable illness — kidney cancer.

The woman could no longer live on her own. The husband could no longer care for her at their home, and instead of leaving her alone to be cared for, he moved her, and himself, into the Alzheimer's ward at a nursing home.

"It was the most selfless act of love I have ever seen," says Nadine. "I realized that, before, I'd lived such a hedonistic lifestyle. Only when I started listening to God did I find a way to make my life meaningful."

Life before the Leap

From Jefferson Starship to Smash Mouth, Nadine was instrumental in the success of some of today's hottest acts. With fourteen gold and platinum records from artists like Stroke 9, Travis Tritt, and Melissa Etheridge, Condon showcased up-and-coming bands like Counting Crows, Third Eye Blind, and Train in the 1990s.

Named as one of the top 100 Californians in the music business, she authored *Hot Hits, Cheap Demos: The Real-World Guide to Music Business Success*. She was the executive producer of a signature event she created and ran: "Nadine's Wild Weekend," Northern California's sole four-day celebration of music. She was also a consultant to music industry bigwigs: BMI, the world's largest performing rights society; Atlantic Records, RCA Records, MCA Records; and CBS radio.

To mirror her professional success, she had a devoted husband, making her life complete. Or so she thought.

The Epiphany of Change

Everything was going along exquisitely. Then in 1999, her mother and her closest friend died.

Nadine felt raw.

"All of a sudden, I was confronted with two people I loved with all my heart who had run out of time," recalls Nadine. "I realized that I had spent my whole career helping a lot of different artists become rich and successful. But I needed to make my life complete."

The desperation to live a life that mattered became an urgent calling.

Providence stepped in. A newsletter seeking volunteers for a hospice program arrived in her mailbox. "I wanted to start to build a spiritual base for myself," says Nadine. "Hospice volunteering seemed perfect. I was at the top of my career. But I found I couldn't ignore this insistent little voice in my head that kept saying STOP. The voice told me that there is more out there than rock and roll."

Standing on the Edge

Feeling skeptical, Nadine remembers driving to the meeting white-knuckled and asking God out loud, "Why are you asking me to do this?"

"I have no doubt I was being called," Nadine remembers. "I mean, I was a cradle-to-college Catholic, and suddenly, I was becoming a menopause-to-death believer."

She experienced confusion and difficulty absorbing "the calling." She recalls how terrified she was en route to her first hospice volunteer meeting, then walking into a room packed with other potential hospice volunteers and being greeted by an energy level and passion that was explosive and contagious.

"I doubted, feared, and freaked out the whole way there, but the second I walked into that room, I knew I had found my people," says Nadine. "I knew I had found my place. Suddenly, amongst all the others in healing work, I felt at home. I knew this is where I belonged."

The reality that she needed to change what she was doing set in. "I had to accept that I was smart, creative, and professional and that I could take all that real-world experience and move on to a world that operated on another level, helping people with what lies beneath the surface," says Nadine. "I knew there was a market for my skills in the business world, but I was about to start dealing with people around end-of-life issues and their spiritual stories as a hospice worker, and that was scary."

The big questions tugged: "Who am I if I'm not the 'Godmother of Rock'?" "What's my job?" "What's my identity?" "How did I honor the lives of my mother and friend?" Helping others with comfort and dignity seemed right.

Nadine gave up trying to find the answers. For nine months — just as if she was pregnant, giving birth to her new self — she waited. She prayed. She meditated. She wrote in her journal. In 2005 and 2006, Nadine continued to mentor rock musicians, but took a paid professional position at the Mission Hospice of San Mateo while she continued to mull her options. "It was hospice by day, rock by night," she recalls.

Then, as if out of the blue, the director at the hospice where she was volunteering quit. Nadine was called in to switch hit, and was named director in 2006.

Suddenly, her personal mission to help those trying to triumph at the end of life became a reality, and she let go of her work in the rock-and-roll world.

"Seeing people run out of time in their lives, I realized that I was smart and creative just like them and that I need to make the most of every day." Nadine says she helps people find creative ways to face death. One woman, tired of everyone asking her about her feelings, asked Nadine to help create a sign that said, "I've already talked about my feelings today. Let's talk about you."

The Liftoff

Another voice was telling her it was time to seize the day and answer the relentless tugging of her soul. Mirroring her gut feeling that she had finally found her place were the words of her mentor and former counselor, Rachel Naomi Remen:

> The most basic and powerful way to connect to another person is to listen. Just listen. Perhaps the most important thing we ever give each other is our attention. A loving silence often has far more power to heal and to connect than the most well-intentioned words.

So she took the job as hospice director in California.

The View from the Other Side

Today, Nadine works full time as a hospice director and in 2007 moved to Phoenix to help care for two ailing relatives.

She never looks back. Her days are spent at the bedsides of people with invasive cancers whom she helps "live toward the end." These moments have transformed her.

How is she different today?

"I realize there is no time today in life for B.S.," says Nadine. "And I also found that the end of life can be very special. People think illness or loss or death is contagious, that if you talk about it you will get it. But I find the most exhilarating people and hopeful people I meet are the ones who face illness or the end of life on their own terms and look forward to every day they have.

"The best times in my life now are when I am with the patients," says Nadine. "I get paid to be kind," says Nadine. "It's incredible. I've never been happier."

Words to Inspire

"I changed," says Nadine. "I realized something. I see broken bodies, people about to die. And what I see are beautiful souls. I am very lucky. I get the honor of relating to and being with people at a very fragile time of their lives. I live a life now that is not about me. It is about them. I am just here to be present to their experience."

Designing Woman

Moving out of pain, Kathy Simonik celebrates her freedom to create a life she loves and redefine what is possible for the students she inspires.

*It is only with the heart that one can see rightly; what
is essential is invisible to the eye.*
— *Antoine de Saint-Exupéry*

Kathy Simonik left a job at a high-powered corporate
advertising agency and turned her life upside down.
Today, as a yoga instructor, she helps others see life
differently — with their hearts.

Kathy Simonik, 52, Barrington, Illinois

Act I: Graphic designer; owner advertising agency.

Act II: Teacher, Anusara-inspired yoga instructor; certified
in scuba diving.

New Script

For all of her success, Kathy was not happy, inside or out.
Chronic back pain and the scare of a fourth and fifth back surgery led to many small, dispiriting moments, and a growing
knot in her gut that said, *It's time to get unstuck.* Her instincts
led her to holistic medicine for a back cure and introduced
her to the world of yoga. Today, she's found a life pose that
allows her to live each day honoring her body, mind, and
spirit. And instead of being imprisoned at her desk meeting
client deadlines, she's guiding a room filled with yoga enthu-
siasts through 10-minute headstands.

Here, Kathy describes her wake-up call and how she
redefined what she's capable of. She reminds us all to pay

attention to the wake-up calls, and most important, to know that it is possible to begin again.

Life before the Leap

The thought of spending the next twenty-five years doing the same work she'd been doing was becoming a pain in the neck and her back — literally — for Kathy. After years of working around-the-clock in the highly competitive, high-rolling world of corporate advertising and running her own freelance graphic design gig, Kathy was exhausted, spiritually and physically. After one stretch glued to the drawing board for ninety unbroken, miserable days, she longed for more days in the garden, where she would flee when the sporadic nature of the freelance biz presented gaping holes in her schedule (and bank account).

Unfortunately, the reality that forces many of us to be stuck — the overhead needed to support our lifestyles — became a noose. Kathy knew something in her live was missing.

"When it was good, the work was good, but there was always a price to pay," says Kathy. "The jobs were super-rush. I often worked late hours. I had been working in advertising for twenty-five years and was making great money but was burned out. I really felt the need to do something more meaningful and life enhancing."

The Epiphany of Change

More alarming was a doctor's advice to have two more back surgeries (she'd already undergone several). The first would be to remove a metal rod that had earlier been run through her spine, and, the second, to replace it with a longer one that would extend into her neck as well. At one point, she had been in a body cast for nine months, and she wore a brace for years.

Standing on the Edge

Seeking alternative medicine, she discovered, not surprisingly, the pain in her back was tension, tension stored up in her spine from years bending over a desk meeting deadlines. "My challenge was to release that tension," she says. She found an alternative doctor who began treating the tissue surrounding her spine. Her mobility gradually increased, and the intense pain faded. She was able to go off the pain medication she'd taken every day for years.

At her doctor's suggestion, she began working with her yoga instructor, Chad Satlow, to strengthen her muscles and increase her flexibility. Today, she can do back bends and headstands.

The Liftoff

Like many of us who are forced to suddenly change our course by accident or injury or life's unexpected moments, Kathy embraced her back injury and transformed it into a blessing. In her fifth decade, she found a gift — acceptance of her lack of control, and a peace and joy in following her heart — and found a place to ask, *What is possible for me, in my life, right now? How can my practice of yoga and meditation help me lead a more satisfying life?* These are questions on which every spiritual seeker and practitioner of yoga and meditation inevitably must reflect.

Yogawerks, the local yoga studio owned by her teacher, practiced a method of yoga known as *Anusara* (a-nu-sar-a), which means "flowing with Grace," "going with the flow," "following your heart." It became the perfect haven for Kathy to explore her second act.

Through yoga, Kathy found herself experiencing more of those cherished times she found when the phones weren't ringing and she could head to the garden to reconnect with the Earth, "and with my soul," she says.

"It didn't come easy," she says. "It's taken four years. It wasn't hard to be dedicated, because I was in so much pain. I was willing to do anything to stop it. My instructor says the most motivated student is the one who wants to move out of pain and into freedom. I'm a living example."

Like many reinventors, Kathy was lucky to find mentoring and encouragement to help make the journey feel less alone and to help her dig deep and tap into the well of strength inside herself. Chad, her yoga instructor, who has grown to be a cherished friend and business partner, pushed her to act skillfully and to not take no for an answer. He continues to be a strong champion and guide for Kathy. She was also blessed to be supported along the way by her husband Jim. "Jim supported me big time and got out of my way while I was trying to transition and figure this out," she says. "At first he didn't completely like it, but gave me the space to be my own person. Huge."

The View from the Other Side

Says Kathy, "I feel like I do make a difference by helping people remember their inner beauty, to realize that our time here is precious and to make the most of every day," says Kathy. "That is the message we try to teach students. It's not just a physical practice — far from it. Yes the body benefits greatly, but once you get tuned up physically, you want to go deeper. That's how I feel anyway, and I can't help but try to instill that in my students and pass that along."

These days, Kathy teaches five days a week at Yogawerks. And she works with private clients herself now and helps them avoid surgery or heal afterward. Several times a year, she embarks on more in-depth training with Anusara founder John Friend. She has completed two levels of teacher training, three yoga therapeutic trainings, Anusara master immersion, as well as more than a thousand hours in Anusara studies. Kathy's teaching style is nurturing and blends her knowledge in therapeutics with a fun, inspiring, and uplifting class. What's more, her husband Jim, who discovered yoga when he observed his wife pursuing a life she had never dreamed possible, also teaches part-time at Yogawerks. After having years of knee and hamstring tightness from his marathon running and general contracting career, he can now see his toes while balancing on the high beam at a building site, says Kathy.

"He couldn't figure out why I wanted to spend so much time on training at the studio," says Kathy. "I think he felt left out. So he started doing yoga and teaches a class now at

Yogawerks. I think it scared him and he wanted to be in on the transformation. It was a good idea. A lot of people go to yoga and start to transform and the spouse doesn't get into it and freaks out."

To let go of the money is hard. "Super hard," says Kathy. "I'm still trying to figure it out. Right now I'm trying to find a balance in my life. I have begun taking more free-lance design again and Jim is doing better with his career. My semi-retiring out of corporate kind of pushed him or motivated him."

Even though she still works a lot of hours teaching yoga at the studio and helping owner Chad launch a line of yoga clothing, the psychological and spiritual aspects of yoga and teaching others to transform themselves through the practice is what Kathy finds most rewarding. She also designed the studio's Web site at *www.yogawerks.com*.

"The cool thing and reason why I'm attracted to it is that it combines my skills with what I love, graphic de-sign and yoga," says Kathy. "It is a natural blend, and if the money was there or when it is, I will be in heaven no doubt. And even though I don't make much money, as Chad says 'I'm rich in spirit.'"

Words to Inspire

"I hope I'm motivating others to work hard to get out of pain," says Kathy. "Not to be on a self-pity mode, but to realize hard work and dedication lead to health. You have to take action to heal."

Getting Started

You want to get unstuck. But how? Here are Kathy's tips for breaking down the barriers and turning dream into reality.

- *Find your inspiration.* "Chad was my mentor. He helped me see my inner light despite all the pain I was in. He encouraged me to become a teacher and changed my life completely." As mentor, Chad also helped Kathy delve deeper into her new calling. "When I started to take private lessons [yoga] from Chad, I instantly felt I wanted more spirituality. I was definitely interested in healing my back, but also felt there was so much more for me."
- *Follow your heart and work hard.* "It took a lot of hard, hard work and dedication. Tons of dedication. I practiced yoga all the time to get strong. Soon the pain was leaving and I was getting stronger."
- *Apprentice yourself.* Find creative ways to work around financial challenges. "To afford the expensive private lessons, I traded with Chad and worked on his advertising materials and designed his Web site. I built up so much trade over the months that he suggested I use the trade to take his teacher training and go deeper into the practice of yoga. I did and that led to me becoming a teacher."

- *Forget the maxim "Do what you love and the money will follow."* Instead, embrace the fact that loving what you do can fulfill you in a way a fat paycheck can't. "Because I was so involved in the yoga, I think the phone stopped ringing in the advertising agency because I was not giving it juice anymore. I had wanted to get out of it years ago and never felt I could walk away from the money. The money was missed, but I felt so much better about myself spiritually and mentally and physically. I was giving back — something I'd wanted to do for a long time."

- *Create a mantra that fuels you.* In the moments when you're not exactly sure where you want to be yet, know that there is a power inside leading you on the adventure. "There's no place like home," is a mantra that Kathy holds close to her heart. "It means to me that everything you need is right inside of you all along. You don't have to go outside yourself to find it."

Making a Difference Every Day

Suddenly the question *What am I going to do with the rest of my life?* looms large. All through our adult lives we have been moving from phase to phase, identity to identity (mom, wife, and executive, volunteer). "Trust your intuition" is the advice we've received time and again when we have made these choices.

Fast-forward to today, as we stand at the threshold of what was and what can be. How do we tap into that inner voice of knowing? How can we make new choices consciously and with courage? No question these moments will be full of confusion and upheaval. But if we rise to the challenge, we will discover the rewards can be amazing.

Step outside the box with these creative ways to try something new and never look back:

1. **Find sanctuary.** Find a place of retreat, where you can step outside the busyness of your life so that you can better relax and recharge your mind.
2. **Find time to take stock.** Ask yourself: What is possible for me in my life right now? What is holding me back? What do I want to change? What do I long to do or be?
3. **Trust your gut.** Following your instincts is more important than ever.
4. **Embrace the feelings.** Understand that change is scary, but realize that these upsetting feelings indicate that we are redefining our lives and shifting from what we thought we should be to who we authentically are.

Get it started. *When* you start matters less than *that* you start.

chapter 3

Begin Again
The power to transform your life is much closer than you realize. Here are some surprising lessons in getting unstuck and on track and to help convince yourself, *Yes, I can.*

Wherever you are is the entry point.
— *Kabir*

Is there something you've always yearned to do, but thought you couldn't? It doesn't have to mean packing up your home, resigning from your job, and traveling to a foreign country to save the forests, although it can be exactly that.

Beginning again is about finding the fire inside of you, the spark that makes your life more interesting, more provocative, productive, glamorous, or upbeat (or at least less sad, dreary, meaningless, and all those other feelings that over time will wear you down).

The reshaping of your life can be something as simple as signing up for a knitting class, or joining a book club, going on Sunday morning bike rides, or trying a new hairstyle.

Suddenly one day you decide to put all the "I can't do it's" to rest, knowing that your life will be more interesting if you did it than if you didn't ever try. It's never too late.

All of us have found ourselves citing reasons — "I don't have time," "It's too hard," "I'm too old"— not to take up something we've always wanted to do. In this chapter we shine the spotlight on those who have hushed those inner voices, tried something new, and never looked back. What they also found was that their personal transformations changed the lives of many others. They spun their passions into saving themselves, and in the long run, made the world a better place for those around them.

In reshaping their lives, they started by taking small risks. And most of them will admit they were scared. They didn't know where to turn. As Henry David Thoreau reminds us, "Not until we are lost do we begin to understand ourselves."

If you want to find what's missing in your life, the best place to start is just to begin.

Finding the Greatest Love of All

Marianne Abdoo turned heartbreak into happiness and a heartwarming tale of love after loss. Coming to motherhood late, this librarian and mom is embracing her new role gracefully and gratefully.

Life changes fast.
Life changes in the instant.
You sit down to dinner and life as you know it ends.
— Joan Didion

It's a scary world out there, especially for those of us in the throes of midlife, standing at the edge of the cliff of what has been and contemplating reaching out and jumping toward what can be.

The more intense our yearning is to make a mark with our lives, the braver we need to be. For many, the fear of suffering a huge pay cut scares them from turning dreams into reality. That's why Marianne Abdoo's story speaks volumes about the gift that comes when we dare to risk. Marianne had suffered great loss in the sudden death of her soul mate and husband, Greg. But she was passionate about making a difference with her life. Here, she shows us how.

Marianne Abdoo, 56, Southfield, Michigan

Act I: Librarian, married to her soul mate, Greg Abdoo.
Act II: Librarian, single mom of two children adopted from
         Siberia: daughter Anastasia, 9, and son, Kuzma, 6.

Life before the Leap

In 2002, Marianne had just turned fifty and was an accomplished librarian, and single, when she reconnected with a former elementary and high school classmate at international folk-dancing classes. The duo became inseparable. "I had not really had a true soul mate in my life," she says. Until Greg Abdoo. They married, set up housekeeping, and began plotting to have a family. The storyline changed when just months later, Greg was killed in an automobile accident while training for long-distance races on his bicycle.

Tragedy entered Marianne's life in the eerily quick way new love had just been ushered in.

"We got along so well, never any conflicts, true respect for each other," says Marianne. "We built each other up too. Greg used to tell me I was so strong. I couldn't believe it. It was very hard for me when he died, just when I had met my guide through life."

The Epiphany of Change

It was after Greg's death that she began to look at her own life differently. Having fallen in love and experienced romance with Greg gave the former teacher turned librarian the courage to pursue a long-held yearning for motherhood.

"It was through Greg that I got my courage to move on and do something with my life. I have a good job as a librarian in a well-to-do community; have been blessed with wonderful parents and siblings and a husband who made me believe in myself. Yet I wanted more out of life. I am a former teacher and wanted my own children if it was meant to be. I grew up in a large family and know the benefits, so I wanted to share that with some children who otherwise would not have had the chance. I never would have thought to adopt these dear children if things didn't happen the way they did."

That's when she started looking into becoming a foster or adoptive single parent.

Standing on the Edge

As a librarian, Marianne specialized in research and looking for and finding resources. She first explored the idea of foster parenting.

"Being a single female working full-time, I did not feel I could give a foster child the attention and support he or she would need. So I went to an international adoption seminar. I found that because of my single status, and my age, there were very few countries from which I was qualified to adopt. I wanted siblings, and fairly young so that there would not be overburdening emotional and psychological trauma already introduced into their lives. I found out that, at that time, Russia was allowing single females over the age of fifty to adopt."

Still, she was skeptical. Her friends and family stepped in, helping Marianne ready herself for the challenge of adopting children from the other side of the world.

"My family helped prepare me by their love and support," says Marianne. "And because of the belief my husband had had in my strength and character, I gained the confidence to undertake this challenge. Not one of my friends expressed one doubt that I would be a good mom."

The Liftoff

Marianne remembers the night she got the call that two children — a five-year-old girl and her two-year-old brother from Siberia who had been abandoned by their parents — had recently been declined by a pair of adoptive parents. She was told the children did not speak English. Marianne didn't know a word of Russian. Moments later, the little boy and his sister's pictures popped up in her e-mail in-box. "Are you interested?"

Marianne, then fifty-two, had fantasized about being a mother ever since she was a little girl growing up in Detroit, the second oldest of six brothers and sisters.

"It was just chance that two young siblings became available so quickly. I have heard stories of people waiting years for their adopted children, and many horror stories of going to get them in their native land and then being denied. I was very fortunate."

She hopped on a plane to Siberia.

"I feel it was meant for me to get these two children," says Marianne.

But she did not get her hopes set on them right away. "I knew that if they had any severe physical, mental, or psychological handicaps, I could not take them. It would not be fair to them. I did not have the time or resources to give to children with those problems."

For several days, she observed the children in their native Siberia. The only way the trio could communicate was through an interpreter. She remembers thinking she had no way to make an accurate assessment.

"They were very excited and did not really pay attention enough to answer directly any questions I asked them. I brought gifts for them — puzzles, picture books, they loved the bubbles, cars for Kuzma, a doll for Anastasia — which they were very interested in, but nothing held their attention very long. These traits they still have today, and I'm very happy they do."

Challenges Back Home

"I only knew a few words of Russian that a friend of mine helped me with before my trip. When we got home, I was afraid they would lose their Russian, so I signed them up for classes at FRUA (Families for Russian and Ukrainian Adoption). However, since no one close to them (family, peers, teachers) speaks it on a daily basis, they lost it.

"When I made the trip to bring them home, we had to stop over in Moscow for paperwork for a few days. I started teaching them a few words at a time — lots of hand motions at first. Anastasia started kindergarten after she was in the United States only a few months. Her English was very poor. Fortunately she had a good teacher who helped in literacy as well as all sorts of social skills. Kuzma went to a day care right down the street — he also had a great day care provider who helped him socialize, learn English, and mature. He had an easier time, since he was younger."

The View from the Other Side

Marianne concedes there were some family dynamics to work out.

"I have learned so much about children who have been deprived of love and care since birth, and this has made me even more appreciative of my good fortune in having a wonderful family and supportive friends," says Marianne. "Although I do not have a vast income, I appreciate my job and the 'wealth' it affords me, compared to the future these children would have had. And I have the pleasure and love of two children who enrich my life daily, despite the challenges and worries about being a good mother to them. I have met many people interested in adoption and have turned them toward further investigation."

These days, Marianne's days are precious — and very busy. She misses Greg very much, but says she is grateful that in the short time they were together, he opened her heart and gave her the confidence to pursue motherhood. Both children are very outgoing and filled with energy that keeps them going nonstop. And, Marianne is at their side, reading books, going for hikes, ice skating, sledding, swimming, and taking treks to museums and parks. Like many suburban American boys, Kuzma loves to try his hand at all things sports. His current roster includes basketball and hockey — a trip to Lake Placid gave birth to his most recent dream to play hockey when he grows up — and he's signed up for baseball. "He's very curious and constantly asks questions about how things work," says his proud mom. He's also into LEGOs and Cub Scouts; Marianne just helped him build his first pinewood derby race car.

Anastasia is all girl. She loves makeup and high heels and would have hundreds of purses if Marianne let her. And Anastasia is a natural nurturer. "From an early age I believe (no real proof except the government took them from their mother for neglect reasons) she was completely in charge of taking care of her little brother," says Marianne. "She has a very strong feeling toward little babies and constantly talks about when she is big and has her own children. She has just recently stopped playing with baby dolls." Anastasia is in Brownies and takes jazz and tap lessons.

"Anastasia is very independent and strong willed," which Marianne attributes to the fact that she had little supervision until age five. But she's adjusting and, under Marianne's tutelage, learning to respect authority and obey rules "because it's the right thing to do — not just for fear of punishment," says Marianne.

School days are especially hectic for Marianne, juggling carpooling and working full-time.

"By the time we get home, I cook dinner and do dishes and do homework with them, it's bedtime," says Marianne. "Anastasia needs a lot of help with homework — she's still working on comprehension and both her math skills and reading need extra attention."

Marianne, who heads her library department, says her biggest challenge is "the lack of time to help my children on a daily basis. We don't have time to relax and enjoy each other in the evenings all week, and I can't go to many school activities during the day."

But the rewards are tremendous.

"My life now is very busy, more stressful than the single life, but more fulfilling," says Marianne. "Every minute outside work is spent in caring for and nurturing these children, trying to make up for the love they missed as infants. They still have so much to learn about life — beyond just physical comforts. But I have seen such progress. I have high hopes for their success in the future."

It took Marianne five decades to make her dream of being a mom come true. But these days, she feels as though she has found her calling and is celebrating the everyday moments of parenting.

The caring goes both ways. Recently Kuzma was kissing her goodnight, when out of the blue he said, "Thanks for picking me out in Russia."

"Anastasia constantly watches me to see what I need," says Marianne. "They both are very thoughtful in their own little ways, running to get me Kleenex when we are watching a sad movie, or setting the breakfast table as a surprise."

Words to Inspire

"I was lucky to get two wonderful children. I know it is a gamble and my life will never be peaceful and calm like it once was. But I consider life an adventure now. Those children appreciate all the small things of life — and that is passed on to me. When I consider what their lives would have been, it makes me all the more grateful for my own possessions and for the love and care I receive from them. It is truly a two-way blessing."

Acts of Faith

Writer summons courage to take a flying leap, seeks out the extraordinary in the ordinary — and lands on her feet.

And the time came when the risk to remain a closed bud became infinitely more painful than the risk to blossom.
— Anaïs Nin

Essentially, it all came down to moxie. Barbara Mahany got serious about putting the pedal to the metal on her dream to start her own blog and have that be the first brave step on her way to create a book.

Barbara Mahany, 51, Wilmette, Illinois

Act I: Pediatric oncology nurse.

Act II: Feature writer for the *Chicago Tribune;* married to the *Tribune*'s architecture critic, Blair Kamin; and the mother of two sons: Will, 14, and Teddy, 6.

Act III: Blog columnist and community leader at *www.pull upachair.org,* "where wisdom gathers, poetry unfolds and divine light is sparked."

New Script

"I dreamed of creating a community, launching a blog and then a book, centered on finding grace in the everyday, in the midst of our homes."

Life before the Leap

For more than a quarter of a century, Barbara has been a newspaper reporter, telling other people's stories. Before that, she was a pediatric oncology nurse who aspired to someday open an inner-city clinic and take care of women and children.

But as the self-proclaimed "chair lady" describes so poignantly in the insightful meanderings on *www.pullupachair.org:* "A sad thing happened on my way to nursing school in Boston. My dad died. At his funeral the priest read a letter I had written to my Papa the Christmas right before he died. Someone who was there — a bigwig at the Chicago ad agency where my dad had spent nearly two decades — took me to lunch two weeks later and said, "Kid, you can write. Have you ever thought of journalism?" I walked home from that lunch, and here, twenty-six years later, I have a master's in journalism from Northwestern, a quarter century at the *Tribune,* a husband and two kids, all thanks to that lunch."

A writing star was born. Still today, Barbara loves her *Tribune* writing. And in the same way she once brought compassion to the bedsides of children and their families, Barbara nurtures her *Tribune* readers with her natural ability to get at what really matters in a story: the crucial capacity, the human heart.

The Epiphany of Change

It was an act of courage to put her musings on the Web. Last year, about to turn fifty, she paid attention to a longing that was just surfacing in her heart, to share her own stories of finding the extraordinary in the ordinariness of her life. Seemingly overnight, she decided to leap, to follow her dream: to create her own footprint with the observations of grace she found woven in the daily living among her family, friends, and the world around her. She wanted to start with a blog, build it to a book, and inspire an online community where others could share as well.

And so on an ordinary Tuesday in December 2007, Barbara just dove in, built the blog, and started writing. She had no business plan. She didn't hire a team of consultants. She didn't do focus groups. And she didn't quit her day job.

She just kept putting one step out there in front of the other and "figuring out where I was going as I went." Her then-thirteen-year-old son Will inspired her courage and newfound Web design skills.

"I figured now is the time. Will told me I could do it, then showed me how, and I did it," says Barbara.

The Liftoff

What Barbara did next was tap into her networks. She test-drove her blog by sending an email blast to friends and family. She invited, "Please pull up a chair. Plop down for a while. . . ." And Barbara started writing — girlfriend to girlfriend, just as if friends were sharing coffee at her kitchen table. Friends wrote back and the conversations started buzz-ing. Today there are about a hundred readers on any given day at *www.pullupachair.org,* and she's counted 20,000 unique visitors.

The View from the Other Side

"I found that by telling my own stories or those of the world right around me — my children, my family — I was able to tap into a level of meaning that lasted," says Barbara. "It held meaning for me, gave meaning to my life, and I had an ink-ling that others might find meaning in the same things.

"I am quite happy to think that many people take the time to make it a part of their every day," says Barbara. "I loved early on when those who comment on the blog real-ized that I was looking for them to share their stories, their beautiful writing and ideas. It became a conversation then, a spiraling up each day. I started it, but the layers of comments and thought took it soaring to new heights, and to nooks and crannies I'd not gotten to."

What's most exciting is that her community has formed its own hub. Fourteen of her most regular readers who share their comments frequently gathered in the winter of 2007 in Barbara's kitchen to meet face to face. One even flew in from Arizona. The "breakfast" gathering began at 10 a.m., and the last visitors walked out the door at 5:30 p.m.

Following Your Passions

In an entry in honor of Martin Luther King Day 2008, Barbara reminds us all that it is never too late to pursue our passions, and that we need to celebrate our freedom to create a life we love.

She wrote in her blog that day: "A year ago, I couldn't imagine being so bold as to put any words here other than the words of the man to whom this day belongs, Martin Luther King Jr. And so, I excerpted from the speech that moves me to shivers down the spine, and tears down my cheeks. I put a spool of words from the 'I have a dream speech' right out on the table, and I let that speak for the day.

"Well, this year, thinking about this day, I am thinking that we must all be bold — especially when it comes to dreams. If we don't reach deep down inside, scout around for that same bold seed, put voice to it, get up and say it out loud, put breath to it, after all, well then, what's the point in only listening to someone else's dream?"

For Barbara, the most rewarding part of her endeavor has been "writing my heart out, being heard, having other voices join in. Finding a much clearer sense of myself and finding great joy in the simplest pleasures in my life.

"I still hope to cull the best pieces, the ones that carry the most meaning to the most readers, and put them together in a book that folks can carry with them to places where they turn for a little quiet contemplation," says Barbara.

Words to Inspire

"I say, if you've got a dream, believe in it, honor it by putting your unique heart, soul, and intellect to it, and make it happen. The only difference between a dreamer and a doer is that little *oomph* that nudges someone off the ledge and into the great winds where change begins. Don't think long term and outcome, just keep taking one solid step after the other, and when you look back you will see how far you've traveled."

Making a Difference Every Day

Crisis and chaos can be key moments of transition. The restless stirrings of unfulfilled dreams that often hit us at midlife, as yucky and sad as they may seem, can often serve the unique purpose of reawakening early dreams and passions. If we are paying attention, these times of transition, upheaval, and sometimes great loss, however painful and difficult, can have a profound way of forcing us to move and grow.

As Marianne shows us in this chapter, we need to let go and take risks to find our true strengths. The more intense the yearning in our lives, the more brave we need to be.

Marianne also reminds us of the gift that comes when we dare to risk.

"Vision," according to English writer Jonathan Swift, "is the art of seeing things invisible." This gift belongs to those who can see the good hidden away in the kernels of setbacks, suffering, and pain. It resides in those who never give up hope.

Here are five tips to help us find the courage to embrace the future:

1. **What do you need to change?** When you are in transition, you may think you need to change everything. But find out exactly what area will help you change your life into what you want it to be. Is it career? A relationship? Your family? Pick the one area that is causing you the most angst. This is usually the one that if changed, will cause the greatest transformation in your life — and help you make a difference in the lives of others as well.

2. **Learn to let go.** Instead of looking back with regret, you can create a picture of what you would like to be, achieve, and experience.

3. **Visualize.** Think about how you will feel, who will be around you, and what the world will be like when you have achieved what you desire.

4. **Set goals in baby steps.** Don't overwhelm yourself with huge, ambitious goals. Ask, what can you do in the next day to start moving toward that dream? The next month?

5. **Push forward.** Start moving toward your goal today. It's important for you to know you are doing everything you can to make success happen.

chapter 4

Reconnect with the Source of Your Creative Spirit
What do you want? What are you good at?
Tap into your hidden talents.

Be strong when you enter your own body;
there you have a solid place for your feet.
— Kabir

Reaching the milestone of midlife can be a very positive experience if you look at this rite of passage as the opportunity and time for exploration.

In 2008, as the first of the baby boomer men and women turn sixty-one and the youngest are forty-four, there is a universe of passionate, educated men and women — married and single — who are unwilling to settle for the stereotypical roles of middle age at the half-century mark. What's best is that they are realizing they don't have to.

We all need role models who show us how not to stay focused on staying young, but to step out and say, "The best is yet to come." We need to ask ourselves, *What am I capable of?* And, we need to make it happen.

The second act reinventors in this chapter advise — by their actions — that the best place to start is by taking an inventory of our own lives. What gives us energy and verve? What do we do to get rid of the anxiety? What are our passions?

Start by making it an adventure to explore yourself.

Going to the Dogs

From public policy activist and economic consultant to co-founder and editor-in-chief of *Bark: A Magazine about Life with Dogs.*

Live your life and forget your age.
— Norman Vincent Peale

It's never too late to realize a dream. Just ask Claudia Kawczynska. After traveling the world and working in a very successful career, she went back to her childhood roots and her simple love of animals and ended up launching a magazine empire. These days, she says she's connected wholeheartedly with the person she was meant to and wants to be.

Claudia Kawczynska, 61, Berkeley, California

Act I: Apple grower, Sebastopol, California; Economic consultant, for Dornbusch & Co. in San Francisco and a Berkeley Waterfront Commissioner.

Act II: Editor-in-chief/Cofounder of *Bark,* a bimonthly magazine about life with dogs that pays homage to the age-old relationship between our two species *(www.thebark.com).* She is also the editor of the best-selling anthology, *Dog Is My Co-Pilot,* and *Howl.*

New Script

At fifty years old, Claudia found her calling. It came with a bark — literally, inspired by her Border collie mix, Nell.

Claudia, who was working as a public policy consultant and traveling with Nell to work at her office in San Francisco's North Beach neighborhood, spent after hours championing the rights of dog owners and their four-legged buddies, advocating for a leash-free area at Berkeley's César Chávez Marina Park.

What began as an eight-page newsletter to spread the cause has found an international audience of dog aficionados. Today, *Bark* has a circulation of 125,000. Claudia is editor-in-chief, and her business and life partner and cofounder Cameron Woo is publisher of the Berkeley-based dog-centric literary lifestyle magazine that boasts a roster of award-winning writers, including Mary Oliver, Ann Patchett, Elizabeth Berg, Augusten Burroughs, Mark Doty, and many more.

Claudia is widely recognized as an expert on dog culture. She has appeared on National Public Radio and has been quoted in *Esquire, Men's Journal,* the *Washington Post,* and the *Philadelphia Inquirer.* This expertise also led to her selection by the *New York Times* for participation on the panel "How We Obsess (Over Dogs)," part of their annual "Sunday with the Magazine" discussion series. She was a recipient of a Hurricane Hero Award from the Humane Society of Louisiana in recognition of *Bark's* Katrina coverage.

Life before the Leap

"I took a very circuitous path to where I am now," says Claudia, who finished college in her mid-thirties, went on to get a master's degree, and then traveled to the Netherlands for postgraduate work; she lived in Paris for the next three years, and celebrated her fortieth birthday there.

When she later returned to San Francisco, she took what she describes as a small job in an economic planning and public policy consulting firm. For five years, she worked on a variety of different projects for state and federal agencies.

The Epiphany of Change

"It was really getting our dog, Nell, that propelled me out of that consultancy life," she remembers. "I was definitely fortunate that I could bring Nell with me to the office, and even luckier that I had a marvelous office off a courtyard in a Maybeck building in San Francisco's North Beach."

Getting Started

It's no secret that many second acts don't get off the ground because those aspiring to create the new get bogged down in the details of the plan. Though business plans and flowcharts and years of planning are regaled by advisors, sometimes you've got to take the plunge and "just do it," agree many successful second act(ers) such as Claudia.

- *Go organic.* *Bark* started organically and grew that way. "The only 'plan' that we had was that it would be a quarterly magazine (to begin with; we are bimonthly now), we would support it through advertising and subscription sales, and, unlike other dog magazines, we decided to never take advertisements from breeders," says Claudia. "We still 'wrestle' with planning. While a business certainly benefits from set plans, and at times I wish we had spent more time in considering various options, it has worked fine for us without that as well."
- *Market yourself.* Claudia and Cameron have never had to invest in expensive marketing campaigns. Word of mouth, and the fact that pet ownership is huge, attracted an audience from the get-go. "*Bark* started to attract readers, advertisers, and others almost from its very start," says Claudia. "There was

nothing whatsoever (and still isn't) like the *Bark* on the newsstands. We are both a cultural and literary magazine, but we are a lifestyle one as well. In 2000 we incorporated, and we received some seed money (not much) for our Web site."

But there was something about "the pull of the wild, or, in my case, the pull of spending more and more time with Nell. Although there were many things I liked about my work, and I certainly learned many valuable skills during my time there, there was something about being called upon as an 'expert' that made me uncomfortable."

Standing on the Edge

There's no question, Nell was the dream weaver. After Claudia and Cameron welcomed their Border collie mix into their lives, they began noticing dogs in literature, art, movies, and poetry. At the same time, they began experiencing the everyday through the eyes of a dog owner. They wanted to let their dog run leashless through the park; for this they needed to rally support from other dog owners. Claudia's daytime job as a consultant came in quite handy when the duo set out to organize the dog group called "Friends of César Chávez Park." And holding the official title of Waterfront Commissioner didn't hurt her credibility in establishing the offleash legislation.

Instead of fearing the fight with city hall, or rather her fellow park authorities, in 1976 Claudia and Cameron handed out about a thousand copies of a newsletter at the Berkeley Marina and left a few stacks at pet stores. *Bark* was born. Initially, the magazine had a smattering of ads from local businesses. But its primary purpose was to drum up support for an offleash area at the waterfront.

The dogs found a romping ground, and the magazine found its niche.

The View from the Other Side

Looking back, Claudia says the calling to magazine editorship was rooted in a friendship she developed in 1967 when she first moved to San Francisco.

"I was lucky enough to befriend a wonderful man, Hirk Williamson," she says. "Back then he was the managing editor of *Ramparts* magazine, and went on to leave them for the fledging music magazine called *Rolling Stone,* where he was the first managing editor.

"Because of Hirk I learned 'observationally' how the world of magazines works," she says. "I learned it was extremely difficult, but with a good idea, and stick-to-it-iveness, one can succeed. It is extremely important to set yourself in it for the long haul."

Stretching Her Boundaries

Claudia also called on achievements she experienced athletically to push herself to create her second act.

"I also learned about staying in it for the long haul because I ran my first marathon at thirty-eight years old," says Claudia. "I loved training for the 26.2 mile race; I learned how to pace myself, how to build up endurance, and how to finish what I set out to do. Hirk cheered me at the finish line of the first race, and he was there also inspiring Cameron and me when we started *Bark*. He died four years ago, just when our first book came out."

A natural risk taker, Claudia also has learned that instead of "believing that it is better to rely on the status quo, I love change. So there really wasn't much trembling there. I figured that if it didn't work out, there were many other projects I could accomplish.

"As a consultant I learned how to assemble expert teams, how to work through processes (many of them political in nature, meaning they required a lot of compromising), and how to work on deadlines. All of those skills came in handy for being an editor. I am very much a do-it-yourselfer — and many of the chores that I had to take on in starting a magazine were very similar to what I have done all my life. I taught myself how to sew when I was ten, by fourteen I was making clothes for my whole family. I was the first organic apple grower in Sebastopol in the '70s [with Hirk Williamson]. I love doing and creating."

What has been most rewarding for Claudia is knowing that what they do has an impact on the lives of dogs and their owners.

"We always urge people to adopt pets from shelters and rescuers, and we have heard from so, so many people about how that message affected their decisions," says Claudia. "We 'elevated' the topic of dog culture, took it out of the show ring, paying attention to the importance of all dogs, no matter what their breed. Also what is rewarding for me personally is the caliber of the authors who have written for us."

Words to Inspire

"I felt like I was entering a 'second act' when I went back to college to complete my undergrad degree — I was thirty-five at the time," says Claudia. "I definitely had a different attitude about myself, in relationship to the other students and the professors. I just loved learning more, understood more fully the importance of learning for the sake of learning. When I started *Bark* (I was fifty), I was perhaps more determined than I would have been if I had done it earlier (like in my thirties). It took me some time to understand what my strengths are and not to belittle them."

A Sweet Escape

Soap opera star turns a pie-in-the-sky inspiration into a recipe for success.

> *I never feel age. . . . If you have creative work, you don't have age or time.*
> — Louise Nevelson

Opening a business can be a family affair and can give everyone in the family a new way to come together.

Just ask soap star Mary Beth Evans, who took her passion for the simple act of baking pies as a way to destress from the glitzy world of daytime soaps and turned it into a national mail-order business.

The recipe: Do what you love.

Mary Beth Evans, 48, Los Angeles, California

Act I: Actress on the daytime soap opera *Days of Our Lives;* mom to Danny, 21, Katie, 19, and Matthew, 16.

Act II: Owner, Mary Beth's Apple Pie Company.

Life before the Leap

Baking apple pies became actress Mary Beth's sweet after-hours escape. Commuting between her Los Angeles home and life as wife and mom of three to New York City for her role in the daytime drama *Days of Our Lives,* Mary Beth turned to her kitchen and the stove to chill out.

The Epiphany of Change

The secret ingredient: a delish pie with fresh, tart apples, cinnamon, and sugar. She started baking them for her family, then for friends and neighbors, and everybody loved them.

She'd been baking up apple pies for years with her own recipe when her husband dared her to see if she could pull off launching her own business. Before long Mary Beth hung a shingle on Mary Beth's Apple Pie Company.

The Liftoff

Mary Beth began simply, by sending flyers around her neighborhood. "For $5 extra, I offered to deliver the pies in my minivan," she enthuses. Upon launching she had one hundred orders.

It was a stint on the home shopping network that threw her hobby out into the universe big time. She sold three thousand pies.

The View from the Other Side

These days she's shipping her frozen and ready-to-go pies across the country.

What she says she likes most about my after-hours biz is "the fact that it role models to my children that moms can indeed turn their at-home talents into success outside the home." But she stresses to them that it takes hard work.

And, at times, it's a family project. "My thirteen-year-old, Matthew, helps me a lot," admits Evans. "He is the fastest apple peeler in the West. He can do a hundred apples in 30 minutes."

Making a Difference Every Day

To refocus our lives, we have to find the clues for what will make us feel good and help others feel good too. Many of us know our talents and the specific skills we bring to our roles as worker, parent, child, student, or spouse. But we have forgotten what we are passionate about. The best way to get in touch with our inner longings is to tap into our creative spirits.

As creativity guru Julia Cameron says: "Creativity is always a leap of faith. You're faced with a blank page, blank easel, or an empty stage. When I ask for help with my creativity, I get it. I believe that there is a benevolent listening something that I have named the 'Great Creator.' I believe that when we ask to be led, we are led, and there's nothing too small or esoteric for spiritual help."

Here are five ways you can get a closer look at where you are being led:

1. **Find your bliss.** Start with an inventory of yourself. What gives you energy and verve? What do you do to get rid of anxiety? What are your passions?
2. **Enjoy the ride.** Look at this search for your inner creative spark as an exciting adventure.
3. **Find mentors.** Make a conscious effort to find people who have already made the midlife leap and are living the "best is yet to come" lifestyle.
4. **Be creative.** Do something you've never done. Mary Beth Evans started baking apple pies. Take a drawing or writing class. Go on a hike. Join a knitting club.
5. **Pray for inspiration and guidance.** Prayer can open us up to guidance, which just renders us ready to listen to our clues, says Cameron.

Dream

**Dreaming of what can be is the catalyst
for us to use our gifts the best we can,
strive for what we thought we never could do,
and learn the power of letting go.**

When people make changes in their lives in a certain
area, they may start by changing the way they talk
about that subject; how they act about it, their attitude
toward it, or an underlying decision concerning it.
— *Jean Illsley Clark*

The rush of fear gripped me as I climbed the ladder, step by step. My toes were perched over the edge of the steel platform. My heart was pounding. I was petrified. Terrified. Of heights. Of recent transition. My trembling was making the platform swoon.

Below, tiny specks of people flailed their arms, cheering me on. I felt like I was going to throw up or die. I focused my eyes on a willow tree across the horizon. I was level with its cradle cap. I sought it out to invoke peacefulness, serenity, and calm. But I was shaking. Worst part: An audience was watching the debut of a public display of my private fears.

I was about to trapeze. I wanted off. *Now!*

I was putting my nerve to the test for one reason: my daughter, Emily. We had come this day to try something new. A group of trapeze artists from the circus was teaching Chicago-area kids the art of reaching out and letting go.

Emily was squinting up at me from the ground below; she'd asked me to be the first to take the plunge. Her only hope was that I could. That I could let go of our past and make that leap of faith into our new future. And make our lives fly again.

"Hep."

I jumped. I grabbed the bar . . . and suddenly I was floating. I was swinging through the air in a lovely dance of freedom. It was truly transforming. Fun. Exhilarating. Floating. Flying. I was flying. I did it. I let go. I wanted to scream from the top of the willow tree. "I did it."

On the car ride home, Emily turned to me and said, "Mommy, I knew you were afraid. But I knew that if you just let go, you could fly."

I use this experience as metaphor to show how sometimes we focus on where we are instead of what wonderful things lie ahead of us if we just let go and open ourselves up to the possibilities of our futures.

In this chapter, a man and a woman who have chased their dreams and let go of what was share their searching, longing, and actions that brought to life their second acts.

Running for His Life

A recently divorced father of two takes on an inspirational journey of perseverance and personal triumph.

> *Pain is temporary. It may last a minute, or an hour, or a day, or a year, but eventually it will subside and something else will take its place. If I quit, however, it lasts forever.*
> — *Lance Armstrong*

Picking up the pieces from the loss of his father, his young son, and a crumbled marriage — a period in which he got out of shape and cranked up his smoking — Bob Daboub found himself at an all-time low. Suddenly a single father to his son, Alex, and daughter, Marie, both in grade school at the time, Bob was determined to jump-start a path to health and happiness.

Like many midlifers who find themselves in the midst of failed dreams and pondering what is next, Bob needed to get one step closer to starting over, but he didn't have a clue what direction to turn in. He started on the path to health and happiness by setting a goal: to compete in the famed Chicago Marathon. After starting slowly — running around his block, then completing two seasons of 5K races — Bob went on to dramatically improve his fitness, which led to him taking on the ultimate challenge and finding his groove both on and off the race course.

In crossing the finish line, Bob also discovered that beyond the race, which is measured by sweat, blisters, and perseverance as well as physical and mental endurance, he inspired others along the way to just get out there. If you want something and are passionate about pursuing it, there are no limitations.

Robert "Bob" Daboub, 50, Palatine, Illinois

Act I: Married, father of two, and couch potato smoker.
Act II: Marathon man.

Life before the Leap

In 1995, Bob was thirty-seven. Newly divorced, he was feeling empty and out of shape. At the same time, he was determined to kick the negative energy and his smoking to the curb.

Bob was looking for a dose of positivity and a way to lift his mood and release stress and tension. He set a goal: to run the Chicago Marathon. "Actually the initial dream was to run a mile without walking or coughing," laughs Bob. "I had been a smoker since sixteen, and needed to stop smoking and get in shape. I wanted to get healthy for myself and my kids — to start over."

Standing on the Edge

Setting a goal is easy. Making it happen isn't — at least not always.

Bob paced his ambition and his training. Determined to realize his goal in the Chicago race, a marathon known throughout the world for its flat and fast course and in which runners frequently attempt to qualify for the Boston Marathon, he started running around the block and then on the indoor track at the local YMCA.

It took him four years to enter his first race: a 5K. "When I crossed the finish line I was so excited, and couldn't wait for my next race." He rose to the challenge, entering three more of the 3.1-mile competitions that were held in Chicago that summer. The next summer he did the same. "My limit was 3.1 miles," Bob says.

The Epiphany of Change

But in the spring of 2001, six years after he set his initial goal, Bob found his running groove, quite by accident, he recalls.

"I was just finishing a 3-mile lap at the forest preserve and I ran into an old friend who was just starting a loop," says Bob. "I told him I would run as far as I could with him. He told me his story of falling in love and marrying his wife while we ran. Becoming so absorbed by his story, I didn't realize I had run 9 miles (three loops of the forest)."

Inspired, Bob started running with the Alpine Runners, a local running club.

"After running with the group a couple of times, they encouraged me to sign up for the CARA [Chicago Area Runner's Association] marathon training program for the upcoming Chicago Marathon in October," says Bob. "It was required that participants already be training consistently at least 20 miles per week. I had not even run a 10K [6.2 miles] at that time; I was running 9 or 10 miles a week and naively proceeded anyway. I pushed myself hard to try to keep up with the group."

The Liftoff

"My family and friends tried to discourage me from doing this. My boss and coworkers just laughed and told me I was nuts."

But Bob was driven to prove them wrong. He pushed hard.

Midway into his training, in June, he developed terrible shin pain and went to his doctor. "My doctor said it was shin splints; however, he wanted to take an X-ray," Bob remembers. "The next day, my doctor called me and told me that I had a stress fracture and to use crutches until I was seen by a specialist. I was on crutches for four days until I could see an orthopedic doctor. He disagreed with the radiologist reading and told me I could start running again. I tried to catch up with the group; however, I was in a lot of pain. I slowly worked up to 10 miles by the end of the month. Lots of Advil and ice."

Too good to be true. In July, the excruciating pain in his legs had returned. Bob was back to the specialist and was ordered to stop running until the results of a bone scan came back. The test results were inconclusive, so the doctor ordered an MRI. Again, inconclusive. Bob was freed from the bench and told to tread lightly.

"By this point it was the end of July, just three months from the race," recalls Bob. "My group had escalated their miles without me. I felt as though my marathon dream was over. I was very depressed for days."

Bob had taken on a major challenge, and he wasn't about to back out now. So throughout August, he practiced every day. But he started with shorter, three-mile runs before building back up to the longer distances.

Very discouraged, he admits, "I felt like I had gotten screwed somehow. Why did this happen to me? After all my work. Now I had to start all over again from a stinking 3 miles. My group was running four days a week with long runs, getting in the high teens in mileage."

Come September, now one month away, Bob was not going to make any more excuses. "I ran 14 miles on September 1; 15 miles on the ninth; and barely finished the 20-miler with my group on September 16," says Bob. "But I was inspired by the group and vice versa. It was great to run with them and start the taper-down miles to race day."

To mentally and emotionally prepare himself for the challenge, Bob scoped out the 26.2-mile race map that showed the marathon course so he could get a clear idea of what the race day would be like. He learned that all challenges, no matter how big, will give you the same result. If you dare. Now he was daring to run a marathon and reinvent his life as he knew it. His biggest obstacle no longer was the nay-saying of friends and family. Now, he was tripping on his own doubts and fears.

"As I was looking at the map, I realized how naive I had been and became fearful that I could not run from Grant Park to Wrigley Field, then back downtown, then west to Greek Town, China Town, and Little Mexico, then to Comiskey Park, then to the lake and back up to Grant Park," says Bob. "I realized it would take hours to drive that distance in a car, a half-day by bike, and I was thinking about running it. How is that even possible? The fear kept me awake at night, and my doctor prescribed sleeping pills because I needed the sleep. I kept thinking that I could not do it, I heard about people dying at marathons, and I heard of a guy who ran with a stress fracture and his leg bone broke in half at the end. I was embarrassed to tell my kids, family, and friends that I was very afraid."

Best Moment
October 7, 2001. Race day.

"The excitement was heightened by the fact that it was less than a month after the 9/11 tragedy," remembers Bob. "Many people who registered did not show up for fear of another terrorist attack. I started the race slowly. It was very exciting seeing the number of runners and crowd."

Somewhere around the 11-mile marker, Bob heard the news that the winner had crossed the finish line in 2:08.

"I was like, 'Okay, we can all go home,'" Bob remembers thinking. "I was exhausted at the half, and the thought of running another 13.1 miles seemed impossible. I needed to keep the voice in my head from making me quit. I just tried to keep up with people in front of me; however, it seemed everyone was passing me and I kept getting slower. They had warned us in the marathon training that the hardest part of getting through a marathon was the internal conversations you would have and how your mind would try to convince you to quit. I guess that's a form of self-preservation. At an aid station just beyond mile 16, I stopped to tie my shoe. When I leaned over, I got dizzy and light-headed and fell over. I needed help to get up and thought I was done. I pressed on one foot at a time. At mile 18 I got a gel with caffeine."

Calling on Divine Intervention

"At mile 19, I went by an old church," Bob says. "I looked up and prayed to God, to my dad who had passed away in 1999 and to my son Brian who had passed away in 1989 for help. I felt a shudder go down my spine, took a deep breath, and made what I thought would be my final push. There were more than 7 miles left to the finish. I started to pick up speed and pass people. The faster I ran the less pain I felt in my shin and knees. As I passed people, I heard jokes about them wanting whatever I had taken."

The crowd was shouting encouragement.

"The crowds seemed to get larger and louder," says Bob. "Coming through under McCormick Place, everyone got really quiet, in into their own heads. I slowed down to talk with a girl who was crying as she ran. She told me she was crying because she missed her grandmother who had just died; she was running in her memory and she did not think she could make it. I encouraged her and told her we only had one more mile. She started to pick up speed."

Crossing the Finish Line

Bob ultimately experienced the marathon in a way never previously imagined.

"When we came out of the tunnel, we were greeted by intense sun and huge crowds cheering and screaming. We could see the finish line. As I crossed the finish line, I was very dizzy and nauseous; however, I was elated. I felt like the race and the training had all been a dream. I kept looking around for assurances that it was real. I finished in 4:28:50."

The View from the Other Side

The next day, Bob could hardly bend his knees and his shin throbbed. He went to a chiropractor who said he had a large calcified lump on his tibia, indicating a stress fracture.

But nothing could stop him now. He had given himself a chance to pursue a challenge and he got out there, discovering how much joy is waiting — in racing and in life.

In 2002, fully recovered, Bob set a goal to run a marathon in less than 3:45. He ran the Chicago Marathon that year in 3:55. He was happy . . . to say the least.

Words to Inspire

"The race wasn't about running as much as it was about me proving to myself that there was something new waiting for me in life — if I didn't give up."

What Bob discovered, and what many of us who take on the challenge of racing also know, is that this tremendously passionate experience involves months and months of preparation, obstacles, setbacks, determination, perseverance, and finally triumph. But ultimately, it is about pursuing your passions in life.

By getting in the race, people like Bob prove to women and men that they owe it to themselves to figure out what is holding them back from doing the things they want in life. By crossing the finish line, they show us that there are no more excuses.

Often the second act includes watching and cheering on those who have been inspired by our actions to push beyond their limitations. Since Bob ran his three marathons, his participation has empowered others to seek the same sense of accomplishment.

"My doctor was inspired and started running to lose some weight," says Bob. "He called me in 2006 to tell me he ran and finished the marathon."

Too often we underestimate the power of a touch, a smile, a kind word, a listening ear, an honest compliment, or the smallest act of caring, all of which have the potential to turn a life around.
— *Leo Buscaglia*

Head of the Class

Mary Graft left a high-paying marketing career to go back to school — literally. Today, she reports to classrooms full of high school students.

If one advances confidently in the direction of his dreams, and endeavors to the life which he has imagined, he will meet with a success unexpected in common hours.
— *Henry David Thoreau*

Mary Graft woke up one day and realized she was living everyone else's dream for her life — except her own. She always dreamed of being a teacher, but instead found herself climbing the corporate ladder, collecting titles as fast as she could climb.

But she'd never yearned for a view from this high up. What she wanted was to help others scale their dreams. She wanted to inspire young people. Instead of having children, as had once been her dream, she wanted to pour her energies into the lives of high school students.

Mary Elizabeth Graft, 45, Palatine, Illinois

Act I: Corporate marketing executive at Sears, Grainger, and the Juvenile Diabetes Foundation; U. S. Peace Corps volunteer, Honduras, Central America.

Act II: High school business and cooperative education teacher.

Life before the Leap

"When I graduated from college in 1984, I was certified in secondary education (social studies), but I went directly into the business world, then got my M.B.A. I longed for children in my life, and fulfilled that by teaching catechism at church and becoming close to my nieces and nephews (all twelve of them). I thought for many years that I would eventually be a mom myself, but I was not blessed with marriage and children, so when I hit forty a few years ago, I started really thinking about teaching."

The Epiphany of Change

Officially hitting midlife, Mary said she realized the advice of sages: "Money does not bring happiness." Her longing to have children in her life was growing stronger and stronger, and after painfully letting go of the idea that she would have her own children, she found that it happened in another way:

she was increasingly drawn to the idea of bringing her maternal skills and her business acumen to the classroom.

"As a hiring manager for so many years, it was clear to me that in some way our public school system was failing us as a society, as we struggled in various markets to find high school graduates who were ready to enter the workforce as contributing individuals," says Mary. "It all worked together to call me to teach business in the classroom, and a job as a cooperative education teacher was the perfect fit."

Standing at the Edge

Cautiously, but with her eye on the prize, Mary inched her way toward her dream. She sent her credentials to the State of Illinois to see what certification she would need. "I was expecting to hear relatively quickly which courses I would need to bring my credentials current." But, nine months later, she was still waiting for her answer.

Not to be defeated, Mary started doing her homework. Instead of waiting, she found a graduate program in education and started taking classes that interested her. She found that she loved being surrounded by other soon-to-be educators, talking about teaching and learning how best to prepare students for their future.

"I networked with whoever I could find in the field of education — spouses of people I knew in the corporate world, my professor and other leaders at my university, friends, neighbors — and listened attentively to their ideas and feedback," says Mary. "When I finally got word back from the state that I only needed one class in special education, I was already on my way to a second master's, and it was easy to sign up for the necessary course at the next semester." She also started checking out how the job market — something she knew a lot about in the corporate world — worked in school districts.

She began her transition strategy.

Good news arrived in the mail. She passed a series of certification exams (so she could be officially qualified across two big subject areas, social studies and business) with flying colors and got her teaching license from the state. The teaching field in Illinois is competitive, but the always overachieving Mary landed the first job she interviewed for — teaching high school cooperative education and marketing at Huntley High School, an hour northwest of Chicago in a rapidly growing suburban community.

Now, came the scariest part. A position as a first-year teacher would cut the salary she received in the corporate world by 70 percent. "In the beginning, my biggest fear was the financial risk: going from making a lot of money to very little. As a single person, I only have me to take care of, so the risk was something I could take on, but it was still scary."

The Liftoff

Providence gave Mary a nudge to quit the business world and start teaching. Suddenly, changes were underway at her company, and her gut and corporate history warned her that at minimum, her position would be restructured. Worse case: layoffs.

"I hedged my bets, and sure enough, my boss came to me with a new organization chart and invited me to join a different team. The company insisted that they wanted to keep me, and then suggested a move to a different department, and I finally suggested we consider parting ways. I was fortunate that the parting of ways included a generous severance package and I already was on my way to a full-time job search as a high school teacher. That very day I received my new State of Illinois teacher's license in the mail. The coincidence felt like fate, or even better, a blessing from God. I was ready to teach."

The View from the Other Side

Today, Mary teaches a marketing class and runs the co-op program at the high school, where seniors leave school early to work at jobs in the community and earn school credit for on-the-job training. With her corporate background, Mary leads the students in engaged "real-life" conversations focused on stories from the front lines of their working experiences and her own experiences in the high-stress world of corporate marketing at industry giants.

She has no regrets. "My days are full and go by quickly," she says. "I knew that I could bring business experience right into the classroom and try to help them. They're really starting to think about the rest of their lives. I'm super-passionate about that."

Mary's students work no less than 15 and no more than 29 hours a week. The students may leave campus early to go to work, and they meet in Mary's classroom every morning at 7:30 to discuss everything from their career goals to how to handle problems on the job.

And, Mary has fallen in love — with her students.

"I have always connected well with kids, and have always enjoyed working with them and being around them," says Mary. "What I wasn't prepared for is how much I would truly just fall in love with so many of the kids. I was shocked during the first parent-teacher night when there was a line out my door the entire night, and parent after parent stopped by to thank me for coming to teach their kids. . . . They told me that I inspired their kids to do well in school or to set good goals for their future, and that kind of feedback was the ultimate in fulfillment."

Words to Inspire

"I spent twenty years at corporations working my way up," says Mary. "I was on a great career path and making good money, but I wasn't thrilled about continuing on that road. I realized it was just going to be more of the same. I decided that teaching would be my way to give back. I knew it was time to move on and find my life's work."

Finding Meaning in Helping Students

When one spends twenty years in corporate America, there is time to think. Lots and lots and lots of time on conference calls, Web casts, workshops, sitting in airports, and meetings, and meetings and meetings.

So, that's what Mary did. She daydreamed about the what lies beneath — the spiritual and psychological under-pinnings of carving out a career during her second act that would reflect her feeling that she was lucky to be living and eager to give back to others.

"I think the fact that I have so much 'real-world' experience and can bring that to the classroom has made a big difference for the kids," says Mary. "Most first-year teachers are right out of college, but I come from a long career in corporate America, so I have stories and experience and wisdom to share.

"It's incredibly powerful to relate a dramatic story to a classroom full of students who hang on every word and are interested in what I have to say, so when that happens it's an awesome feeling and reinforces that I did the right thing.

"Also, when I know I've made a connection with a student in some way, it's like God reaching out to me to remind me that I'm in the right place. On Christmas Day I heard from six different students who just called to say, 'Merry Christmas, Miss Graft!' That was incredible. . . . They think of me on their winter break? Yes, and that always seems to impress me because it is evidence that I am making a difference in their lives."

Making a Difference Every Day

Knowing what is missing in our lives and how to find it is a bit of a challenging puzzle, to say the least. Many agree that the power to transform our lives is much more attainable than we can even imagine. But let's face it — there are a zillion voices in our head that discourage us. "I'm too old."

"I've got three kids in college and can't afford to go back to school." "What makes me think I could run a marathon, or launch a foundation to help others who are experiencing the cancer that I have survived?"

"We have a place of fear inside of us, but we have other places as well — places with names like trust and hope and faith," says Parker Palmer. "We can choose to lead from those places, to stand on ground that is not riddled with the fault lines of fear, to move toward others from a promise instead of anxiety."

Here are five ways to hold to and go after the newness of promise:

1. **Follow your heart.** There's a famous line in the movie *Field of Dreams:* "If you build it, they will come." This was a message from the baseball gods to Ray Kinsella (Kevin Costner) telling him to build a field in the middle of the Iowa cornfields. Even though everyone else told him he was a crazy dreamer, sure enough, Kinsella's baseball field became a spectacle, attracting paying crowds from far and wide. All of us need to tap into the Ray Kinsella inside ourselves.

2. **Set a timeline — now.** We sabotage our own dreams with "someday" timelines and waiting for circumstances to kick into gear. There is no finish line or finished state. There is only now. Tomorrow is now.

3. **Take a risk.** Don't wait or pray for things to happen, believe in yourself, tap into your own confidence (even if you have to pretend for now you have it), and take action.

4. **Remember pain is temporary.** In this chapter, Lance Armstrong reminds us that pain only lasts for a while. But if we quit, it will last forever.

5. **Call on divine intervention.** Sometimes, when we feel we just can't make it one more step, we need a power higher than us to turn to and ask for that final push. A friend of mine, Sandy, puts the names of people who have made a difference in her life and whom she wants to honor, on twenty-six separate scraps of paper when she is running marathons. She pulls out a name for each mile, calling on that special person in her life to help guide her and to muster the courage and strength to make it to the next mile marker. What you are dreaming for lies just around the corner. Don't give up.

chapter 6

Identify the Next Steps
Do your homework. Ask for guidance — within yourself, and through the research you do. Listen deeply. Solutions emerge where the questions are posed. So ask, *What next?*

It's not the answer that enlightens us, but the question.
— *Eugene Ionesco*

Midlife is not a crisis; it's a time of rebirth, according to best-selling author and lecturer Marianne Williamson. Indeed, the need for change as we get older is a powerful one. We're at a time in our lives when a lot of the old ways of being are gone. Our kids are growing up. Our relationships are being challenged. We can dwell on these transitions as loss, or we can embrace midlife as a chance for something new to be born.

Second act reinvention in itself is big. But, no matter what reinventions are, they are change. In this chapter we look at individuals who are exploring ongoing changes and have made some that, to the outside world, may not seem momentous. Nevertheless, by acting on their dreams, they have become role models for themselves and for all of us.

Turning Points

The splendor of Acapulco and the challenge of rafting the rapids helped Lois Coldewey leave her marriage, her career, and life as she knew it — and reinvent her future.

> *When the time is ripe, the vision will come.*
> *— Joyce Rupp*

Lois Coldewey spent much of her adult life married and raising her two children. She became a part-time student working on a master's degree, a process that took twenty-three years. After that, she worked in a variety of health care specialties, from medical and surgical positions to psychology, faith partnerships, administration, community outreach, and cancer support.

Lois Jean Coldewey, 65, Des Plaines, Illinois

Act I: Wife and mother of two grown children, Michael and Tracey; grandmother of three, Rachel, Sean, and Danny; registered nurse.

Act II: Spiritual director, pastoral holistic nurse, and healing touch certified practitioner.

Life before the Leap

Lois's marriage was not fulfilling, and she yearned for a career that would make a difference in the world. Her own illness pushed her to give back and become a champion for others navigating illness and loss. Lois harnessed the loving energy from her years as a nurse and mother and became a spiritual director and healing touch practitioner.

The Epiphany of Change

The biggest transformation in Lois's life started as a fluke. In 1997, she was just about to turn forty, had recently recovered from heart surgery, and was on vacation in Acapulco with her husband. Lying on the beach and soaking her senses with the sound of the surf slapping the shore, the soft, gentle breezes, the warm sand, and the lapping waves, she experienced a misty, mystical moment.

Lois was grateful for her health and happy to be alive, but her marriage was shaky, and she felt a restlessness to find deeper meaning and awakening and insight into what lay ahead. "I had just recovered from many health problems, and I knew life wasn't infinite," says Lois. "I wanted to thank God for getting me through." Lois seized the opportunity to issue a fundamental plea: "God, send me a sign for a way I may say Thank You to you for my life. . . ."

Suddenly, before she had even finished her query, a hang glider passed above. She remembers saying, "Oh no! Please, not that." Even though she loves the ocean, she's not a swimmer; she fears encounters with sharks, and heights terrify her. She had no intention of taking up hang gliding. But she surrendered to the metaphorical significance of the moment.

Standing on the Edge

"The Spirit's call was as intense as the fear, and I realized that in facing my fear, and trusting in the source of all life, I would indeed honor life," says Lois. In late 1997, she became a nurse. That began her odyssey into fundamental questions on how to live her life, and a scary journey of self-reckoning that would shape her next two decades.

The question that would guide that journey: "Tell me, what is it you plan to do with your one wild and precious life?"

Lois's midlife journey would be exactly that — wild and precious, she now laughs in reflection. Today, she defines her second act as "She Who Listened," in contrast to her previous outlook on life, "She Who Is Much Afraid."

After returning from her Mexican vacation epiphany in 1983, Lois knew she needed to start reinventing her life. But she concedes she dipped her toes in slowly. She continued to work on herself and on her marriage, joined Al-Anon to help cope with and understand her husband's alcohol addiction, entered a chaplaincy program and pastoral studies master's and, while raising her kids, went to school and pondered her next steps. "I don't think any of this affected my kids because I still did everything and I studied quietly in my bedroom," recalls Lois.

The Liftoff

The huge leap came when Lois took a job as a parish nurse for $10,000 a year. In 1998, she separated from her husband and lived "very frugally." She roomed with a woman she'd met at Al-Anon for six months. When she and her husband divorced in 1988, she moved back into their house, but she sold it shortly afterward and bought a condo — "My first independent purchase," she says.

"I felt like God had called me into new life, like an IV transfusion," says Lois.

A Circle of Friends

One way she chose to celebrate the milestones — her new determination, patience, facing her fears, and hard work — was to invite the support and encouragement of friends.

Lois began using parties and birthdays as celebrations of the new joy she was tapping into. One thing she could control amidst all the transition was what she did on her January 8 birthdays, so she began using them as launching pads for what lies ahead. "I've always tried to create some way of honoring the day I was given the gift of life."

For her fiftieth birthday, in honor of celebrating her conquering of another life-threatening health event — cervical cancer — Lois was reminded again of her beach promise to risk more and have more fun. She wanted to, as she explains, "express my old broad" years, so she held a bash and dubbed it, the "When I'm an Old Woman, I Shall Wear Purple" party. She and her friends dressed wildly, told bawdy jokes, and even "practiced spitting" in the snow. She then traveled to Sedona, Arizona, alone, and took a "hot air balloon trip" facing another of her fears — heights.

"I went on to take more risks, be less afraid, and value the rich life experiences that I had and continued to say 'yes' to," she says.

At fifty-two she joined nine other women in a rapids-rafting trip on the Colorado River, calling the trip "Twenty Boobs in a Boat."

They say that rafting the Colorado River changes you. Running rapids brought a realization. "Talk about facing fear! I had many incredible and harrowing experiences. One story is when the little river came up on the shore and swept me away!" Surviving and seeing the vast beauty of nature was its own reward.

From that trip she carried away a metaphor for her newly created life: "The river (life) sometimes sweeps you away even when you think you are not ready, and the river holds you through it," reflects Lois.

"A year later, as I reached age fifty-six (the official age of 'cronehood'), I gathered many wise women around and we explored and celebrated life's learnings," Lois says. Their strength supported her through a "job downsizing," which left her no choice except to launch her own touch practice.

Recently, for her sixty-fifth birthday, she gathered friends for an afternoon of her "Awake: A Celebration of Living." She offered this tribute to her own life: "I have a heart full of the love of family and friends, and I know that I can face whatever comes."

She had a friend compose a song for the event: "It's good where I've been and it's good where I'm going."

The View from the Other Side

Fast-forward to today. At sixty-five, Lois makes her living as a healing touch spiritual minister and spiritual director, giving retreats for women that help guide them to ask and answer for themselves some of the same deeper questions of meaning that Lois has explored. She has sought out a contemplative life, and she helps guide others to a life that unites them with both the Creator and creation.

As a healing touch practitioner, she works with cancer patients and many others who are dealing with terminal illness, along with individuals seeking emotional and spiritual wisdom, courage, and comfort.

Biggest Hurdle

"Facing my many fears was huge," says Lois. "I feared physical danger, failure, the end of my identity, many relationships, dreams, a total unknown, the 'road less traveled' in my career, and at the same time I was battling some significant health crises," she says. "To get through, I tapped into my deeper spiritual place for strength and courage."

Throughout the years, she has come to embrace risk taking as a teacher of many valuable lessons.

"Every day I can celebrate the authenticity of my life," Lois says. "I've gained confidence in following my inner voice and learning to trust in my ability to live life according to my values. But mostly it is the chance to use my gifts to make a difference in the world. *Life* is a great gift. It is very rewarding to be able to help someone challenged by life's circumstances to change what they can and accept what they can't and to live life fully."

What's Next?

"And now, at sixty-five, I'm finally completing my 'Five Wishes' (a living will with heart), beginning Social Security, and facing my physical mortality once again (probably heart surgery). I pause to focus on quality of life, acknowledging what has been, letting go of what is no longer, accepting more of who I am and who others are, and going forward to cherish the future present moments.

Words to Inspire

"I hope I am a healing presence in the world, empowering others to see their goodness and what is right versus wrong, through compassionate listening, belief, and resources. I work in a partnership model — 'I/Thou and Spirit.' Whenever I ask about my life 'purpose,' the answer is always 'Just love' (and let go of the outcome)!"

Embracing Midlife

This fearless woman grabs for the reinvention rung to create new life after the working-mom track

> *Education is not the filling of a pail, but the lighting of a fire.*
> — *William Butler Yeats*

At age fifty-four, Pam Mitchell — married in her twenties, now a mother of a young adult daughter and a son in high school, and caregiver for her aging parents — finds herself reexamining choices she has made, including her profession and what she wants to do with the second half of her life.

You don't spend nearly thirty years on the working-mom track, balancing a busy career as educator and raising two children, without learning carefully how to navigate your next move. But sometimes, you've got to do what you've got to do.

Pam Mitchell, 54, Inverness, Illinois

Act I: High school and college biology teacher; mother of two children, Will, 16, and Susan, 24; wife to Bill.

Act II: In process.

New Script

"I would like to use my educational and biological backgrounds in new ways, as a volunteer tutor or as a degreed and certified genetics counselor. I am looking into volunteering for the Jesuit volunteer corp and beginning graduate programs in genetic counseling."

Life before the Leap

Pam was an accomplished college and high school biology teacher with a daughter about to graduate from college and embark on a nursing career and a son entering high school. Pangs of the impending empty nest began to creep into her life script, forcing her to begin considering the what-ifs. "What if I go back to graduate school? What about full-time volunteering?"

"I wanted more flexibility than my full-time job gave me," says Pam. "Also, I wanted to do something that would give back to the world."

The Epiphany of Change

Suddenly crisis struck, but not in the form of the midlife version. A car crash would give Pam months and months of time in a hospital bed to reflect on her second act — and remind her of the adage to live each year as if it's your last. Just a week before her daughter, Susan, would be graduating from college in the spring of 2006, Pam and her husband, Bill, were driving on a rural road near their Wisconsin vacation home when they were broadsided by a truck.

Standing on the Edge

She would spend the entire summer in the hospital with internal injuries as well as damage to her legs and shoulders. Her husband sustained only minor injuries. With the wonderful care and concern of endless medical professionals, family members, and friends, Pam's numerous injuries, surgeries, and rehabilitation gave her the incentive to renew her faith in humankind and to appreciate each new day. It also prompted her to think about paying back, doing for others what had been done for her. When she couldn't get to a therapy appointment, she called on the local FISH (For I Shall Help) organization for a ride. (Now she is a regular volunteer driver for that group.)

Pam found herself reexamining old dreams and creating new ones. Some were dreams she had talked herself out of fulfilling because, at the time, she was caught in a balancing act between what would be good for her family versus what she would like to do.

One thing she knew for certain is that she wanted to incorporate her innate drive, passion, and previous years of experience as a teacher with a willingness to learn anew with a relaunched career and life purpose. Pam is finding a lot of pleasure and a challenge in pondering the different options for what could lie ahead. What's easy is knowing she wants to follow her passions to carve out a new path.

"With my children moving on with their lives and at my husband's career stage as he heads closer to retirement, I want more flexibility to travel, and I have a keen desire to do something new (not just be a pampered, stay-at-home socializing and shopping suburban woman)," laughs Pam. Having taught at the college and high school level for twenty-seven years, teaching is no longer on her list of "someday I'd love to."

"I loved teaching college biology at Harper [a suburban Chicago community college]," says Pam. "But I was ready for something different. I have affected many lives with my teaching, and I want to keep leaving my mark. Joining a volunteer group or going back to grad school would be new challenges."

The Liftoff

With the Internet at her fingertips, Pam is savvy about doing research. She spends hours researching for her "next" opportunity and studying others who are successful. She is tapping into the journeys of mentors for guidance and example. One is a friend from her community who commutes to Chicago's inner city to work with the Jesuit volunteer corp. Another is Ricky Lewis, author of the textbook *Human Genetics* that Pam used to teach in her college class. Ricki "has built a multifaceted career around communicating the excitement of life science, especially genetics and biotechnology," and provides an excellent role model for Pam.

The View from the Other Side

"I've tried shopping, spa visiting, lunching, etc., and I feel purposeless," says Pam. "I cannot just do this. I need to do something important, using my gifts and abilities.

"I am trying to be cognizant of what I can do for others. I've been on the receiving end for so long it's my turn to be able to give something back. I have been volunteering for FISH, driving individuals with special needs to doctors' appointments. And when friends' children are struggling with their science classes, I have tutored and guided them through tough tests and finals."

She adds, "Working in the campus ministry office at my son's high school gets me back into the school scene and reminds me how vital, exciting, and fast paced it is. I am also working hard on an alumni committee at the high school to help reestablish the connections and involvement that I have

Be a Shadow for a Day

What do you want to be when you grow up? Teens play that all the time. Shadowing is just like it sounds. You follow someone around watching what he or she does. With the easy resource of the Internet, you can do some research and see if there are professional associations or groups in your area of interest. Often, they will know of educational or mentoring programs for you to contact and see if you can shadow someone for a day. Also, network. Let your family, friends, and friendly colleagues know you are interested in exploring this new arena. Often they will know someone you could contact to ask what it is like and to ask if you could shadow them.

so greatly benefited from. I also continue to offer guidance to colleagues at the college when curriculum issues arise. I cannot totally step away."

Making a Difference Every Day

When we get to the point where we feel we have hit the wall of void, the total absence of meaning in our lives, what do we do next? How do we identify our path? How do we know which step is the right one, and which will lead us in the wrong direction?

1. **Identify what you need to give up.** What are you willing to give up to follow your dream? Could your modest lifestyle be made even more modest? Examine which material 'needs' and 'wants' are less compelling to than your dream.

2. **Do your homework.** Let your fingers do the walking on the Internet. With the Web as one of the fastest and most resourceful research tools in town, you can soak up a lot of information fast. For example, if you're hoping to launch a new business, you can quickly scope out competitors. Interested in eco-travel? Check out the travel Web sites. Everything you need to know is in front of you.

3. **Start slow.** Before you take the big leap, test-drive your idea. If you are launching a pie business, bake a few pies before you start mass market producing and trying to sell them. Looking to dive into a business in swim coaching? Reach out to athletes and health clubs in the area and experiment by holding a few coaching sessions.

4. **Look for signposts.** When you announce to the universe (and to yourself) that you want to move in another direction, small and subtle things and people will start appearing on your path. Lessons arrive when we are ready for them. Pay attention, follow your heart, and you will learn everything you need to know to move forward. Signposts lead us to some pretty unexpected — and wonderful — places.

5. **Muster the will to achieve it.** The distance to our next place, to reinventing ourselves, is usually much further than we think. But, remember, change is the result of our attitudes. Stay positive — where there is a will, there *is* a way.

Find Your Personal Best
Ask yourself, *What am I capable of?*

Pursue things you really love doing, and do them so
well that other people can't take their eyes off of you.
— *Maya Angelou*

No question, it is important to find a passion and chase it.
Whether you bake bread, paint murals, or aspire to cycle like
Lance Armstrong, you'll redefine yourself in your own eyes.
When you're on a mission because you have the courage to
act on what you value, you are in your zone. You know it.
Others know it.

If you are truly serious about second act reinvention, nothing and no one will stop you from doing what you love. It
might take small steps: teaching a spin class at the YMCA at 5
a.m. before your 9-to-5 job; writing the book on weekends;
or volunteering at the food kitchen after hours. And when you
do what you love, people will notice. It's contagious. "You've
got to find what you love," says Steve Jobs, founder of Apple.

In this chapter, these second act reinventors underscore the fact that if we pursue what we love, we can't lose.

Making a Splash

Lawyer dives back into his first love — the water.

> *A calling is a sense that your very being is implicated in what you do. You feel that you fit into the scheme of things when you do this particular work. You have a sense of purpose and connection in the work. It defines you and gives you an essential tranquility. Toward the end of your life you may see all the jobs you have done as fateful, composing your life work and answering your calling.*
> — *Thomas Moore*

In the rising world of triathlons, athletes bunch together tightly in open water, forming a pack and elbow-throwing and splashing toward the finish line. Then, they climb onto dry land, strip off their goggles, wet suits, and bathing caps, don helmets, hop on cycles, sprint again, hop off, and then run to the final finish.

Triathlons have been called much more than a sport in motion; they're a metaphor for all the little and big things that matter to a person who's reaching for new goals.

For many, like Drew Surinsky, they symbolize what it takes to jump into your second act and swim, run, and cycle in a new race for yourself, for your new life.

Drew Surinsky, 43, St. Louis, Missouri; Boulder, Colorado; and Evanston, Illinois

Act I: Attorney (assistant public defender).

Act II: Exercise physiologist, strength and conditioning coach, triathlon coach, and swim coach.

Life before the Leap

Guys like Drew of Evanston, Illinois, can attest that triathlons can be a personal reminder that tackling a new goal in life can be just as terrifying as plunging into open water and often means starting from scratch — but that nothing feels better than crushing a new learning curve.

That's what happened when the then-thirty-five-year-old St. Louis native decided to shed his three-piece pinstripe and pursue his dream to help people become stronger. His real passion was swimming and coaching in the pool.

Prior to graduating with a law degree from the University of Illinois, then working as an assistant public defender and research and contract attorney, Drew had always worked in aquatics and fitness. In high school and college, he could swim faster than most people ever hope to.

But, as he grew more mature, it was time to pick what he thought he had to pick — an "adult" profession — and he majored in philosophy and choose law because it was something he had to prove he could do. And as a public defender, he felt that he could help a few people.

"I couldn't stand being a lawyer," says Drew. "I left work every day feeling awful, and it got progressively worse and began taking a toll on my health and mood."

Standing on the Edge

To cope, he swam.

"After every workout, I'd remember how it didn't feel awful after leaving work at the pool, and I'd say to myself, 'God, I wish I still worked at the pool.' I kept thinking I wanted to make a living by helping people to become physically stronger. It's a bonus that I can do it in the water."

Struggling to reenergize himself every day, he decided not just to dream about a career training others to be fit. Instead, he chose to train himself to end "my suffering and undue misery."

The Epiphany of Change

To inspire himself, Drew turned to another one of his passions — drumming — for a motivational boost. For him, the role model was Max Weinberg (drummer with Bruce Springsteen and currently the drummer and bandleader on *The Conan O'Brien Show*).

"I had read an interview where Max was talking about the years in the early '90s, when Bruce broke the band up for a while," says Drew. "Max was getting depressed and wasn't sure what to do with himself. He tried law school for a while, but he didn't like it, and he was starting to lose some of his drumming chops. He decided that he needed to drum more, so he just started practicing a lot, even though he didn't have any great prospects at the time. He had this *Field of Dreams* mentality in which he decided that 'if you drum it, they will come.' Of course, Max Weinberg is now more successful than ever, and that leap of faith that he took is a source of cautious inspiration for me."

Drew discovered that the steps to change would not happen overnight, but rather were a "gradual process," one that took place over the course of ten years.

The Liftoff

At the time, he and his wife, Anne, had just moved to Boulder, Colorado. He seized the opportunity to practice law only part-time as a researcher and started his own business, opening a flotation tank center, working several jobs at local pools, including a hospital therapy pool.

"Our four years out there gave me time to decompress as well as to see that there are 'adult' careers in fitness and wellness," recalls Drew.

When the couple returned to the Chicago area, Drew was planning on becoming a physical therapist. He says, "I ended up becoming an exercise physiologist and coach, but more important is by the time we were back in Chicago, I was convinced that there were livings to be made in a field I didn't hate."

Drew went back to school, earning a Master of Science degree in exercise science and certifications as a coach and personal trainer.

"It happened fairly organically," says Drew. "I talked to friends of friends who were doing related things in health fields to get a sense of what I thought I wanted to do. I knew it was going to start with becoming a personal trainer and then with school. I studied for a few months for the personal trainer certification and found fairly healthy demand. From there, I continued personal training while making up undergraduate prerequisites and then getting the master's in exercise science. I also got other certifications such as triathlon coach and swim coach."

The View from the Other Side

These days, Drew competes in his own triathlons. He says, "I started doing triathlons in 1987, and it was a good fit for me from the beginning. I've done seventy-something races at distances from sprint to half-Ironman, and I have even won a few small-time ones." He also coaches both private and group sessions at several Chicago-area facilities and training programs. Since becoming a certified triathlon coach in 2000, Drew has coached hundreds of athletes, ranging from children to seniors and from beginner to elite athletes.

His typical day might start with a few private sessions, meeting his wife Anne for a midday workout, then heading out again to coach a group workout and more private sessions. He also spends many weekends leading swim technique clinics for competitive triathletes and beginner workshops for the aqua-anxious, spending five hours on a Saturday afternoon coaching reluctant triathletes to take the plunge and get in the pool.

Other than Anne, Drew says what he loves most about his second act is "that I have a career that matches my temperament and talents. I have a lot of independence and flexibility. My job is largely about the relationships my clients and I forge with each other and the intellectual, creative, and emotional effort that I contribute. Unlike being a lawyer, I'm working largely with clients who are happy to see me."

Finding Joy in Helping Others Meet Their Fears and Pursue Their Dreams

What makes it the most rewarding, Drew says, is the true joy he finds in help people overcome barriers and accomplish goals that are deeply meaningful to them. "The neat thing is that by hiring me to help them, they're also helping me do the same," he adds.

His advice for others looking for a second act? "Explore, pure and simple."

Eventually what pushed Drew to take the risk was convincing himself that he could make a living in fitness. And, he says the support of his wife Anne convinced him that he could do it.

Words to Inspire

"Staying healthy and gradually feeling good about the idea that it's OK to not be a lawyer, was a great moment. It's also been nice to be able to gradually 'trust the world' more that there will be people willing to pay for what I provide."

Taking the Ride of a Lifetime

Sixty-five-year-old colon cancer survivor from Barrington, Illinois, rides his bicycle 6,500 miles across America to help find cures for cancer and ALS (Lou Gehrig's disease) and to help promote awareness for hospice care.

To travel hopefully is a better thing than to arrive.
— Robert Louis Stevenson

Many second act reinventors use their birthdays as markers. When Bob Lee was turning sixty-five, he celebrated his milestone by riding his bike across the country and raising $130,065 each for three causes: the Les Turner ALS Foundation, the American Cancer Society, and the National Hospice Foundation for Public Awareness. In 2008, he was named the recipient of the Les Turner ALS Foundation's Hope through Caring Award. He'd dreamed about riding his bicycle across the country, but he'd spent most of his life in a three-piece suit at the helm of a boardroom.

Bob Lee, 65, Barrington, Illinois

Act I: Father of two grown children; grandfather of six; president of Eastern Standard Corporation, and career-long senior corporate manager.

Act II: Philanthropic sojourner and fund-raiser.

New Script

"I wanted my challenge to be riding solo, to see if I could motivate myself to do that," says Bob, who had made a similar cross-country trek once before, raising funds for charities as well. "But I quickly discovered that I was sharing the journey the whole way along the way. I met thousands of people along the ride, and each of them had a story that inspired me to reflect on many things and on how I was using my life."

Ask Bob, a colon cancer survivor, if age or illness are excuses to slow down, and he'll whip out a photo album and direct you to a Web site filled with his experiences and the people he met along the way. His journey will leave you huffing and puffing to find a way to inject purpose and meaning into your own daily living. He calls his ride a metaphor for his personal journey from success to significance.

Life before the Leap

Twenty years earlier, at age forty-five, Bob started getting the itch to do something, anything, beyond his corporate life. That's when he started incorporating physical challenges. He started with 10K races and triathlons and pursued his interests in photography and gardening. He started thinking about redirecting his career path away from the boardroom and toward "a purpose-driven life."

The Epiphany of Change

His epiphany moment to reach out was inspired by a former neighbor who had ALS and by reading *Tuesdays with Morrie* by Mitch Albom. "I decided to give back through a fund-raiser to find a cure for Lou Gehrig's disease and raise awareness for hospice."

Standing on the Edge

While Bob never had a million-dollar nest egg to finance his second half, he says he managed money well so that he would be able to pursue his passions, and more important, take what he loved doing — cycling — and find a way to pursue significance with that without "causing my family to starve."

"I always knew I wouldn't be able to live off my retirement, so I made sure I set money aside in savings," says Bob. "As I approached retirement, I had this hollow feeling. 'What am I going to do that makes a difference?' Retirement clearly wasn't for me. I had enjoyed success and wanted significance."

The Liftoff

Bob developed a plan. He decided he would retire at fifty-eight and started making a list of everything he wanted to do. "I had no idea where I was heading," he recalls. "What I did know was that I had gotten myself pretty fit physically, loved that feeling of athletic challenge, and I'd always dreamed of getting in an RV and traveling the back roads."

All the pieces of the puzzle seemed to fit: Why not ride his bike across the country and do it for the causes he wanted to commit his energy to? Appropriately he dubbed it "A Ride for 3 Reasons." He would raise money for ALS, hospice, and cancer, having been a survivor himself.

"It was perfect because I got a lot out of the biking—the solitude and yet meeting wonderful people along the way—but I also got great satisfaction in knowing I'm helping people who suffer from horrible diseases."

Dubbed by some as Bob "Gandhi" Lee, the guy is unstoppable. He hopped on his bike on March 29, 2007, in Jacksonville, Florida, and didn't stop until September 6, 2007, when he reached Bangor, Maine. Along the way, he stopped at Ground Zero in New York City, the Pentagon, Superstition Mountain in Scottsdale, Arizona, and the Gateway Arch in St. Louis.

The View from the Other Side

"I got to see everything I'd dreamed about seeing," says Bob. "Most important, I realized that aging doesn't have to be about facing a void. Actually, all you need to do is examine what you really love to do, do it, and somehow something spectacular will open up for you. I realized that if I didn't become roadkill on this trip, I would be doing something pretty significant."

Bob's motivation to keep on pedaling uphill is the people he's met along the way. One in particular is Aimee, a thirty-eight-year-old mom of three young children, who has ALS.

"On a tough day when my stamina was taxed, I thought of Aimee, and then I would go back and look at what I am doing with my life, and how lucky I am to have made it to forty and beyond," says Bob. "We need to start looking at forty as a marker to say, 'Wow, there is so much more I can do with the rest of my life. What will that be?'"

Bob is a living billboard for doing good. To those who know him, he is the doorway that leads into the world where it always feels good when you are doing good.

Words to Inspire

"My hope is that along the way people saw what I was doing and see that there is something they can do to help others back home in their communities."

Making a Difference Every Day

You're now at the point where you have made a profound commitment to your reinvention. When there is no turning back, it is time to concern ourselves only with moving ahead. But how do we silence the negative voices on the sidelines? Where do we find patience and persistence when there will always be solid reasons not to move ahead? It's time to start uncovering what the world wants of you, and the tools for finding the courage to say "yes" to your new life. One strategy that works is to conduct a personal assessment of your life so that you can push your personal best into your new future. Here are five questions to ask yourself:

1. What are the roles you currently play and what do you do really well? What is missing?
2. What are the parts of your personality that have disappeared or been put on hold?
3. What used to make you feel passionate? For Drew it was swimming.

4. How would you feel if you could do those things again?
5. How can you bring your personal best, your passions into your life again?

From *Tuesdays with Morrie*

On Getting Meaning into Life

"So many people walk around with a meaningless life. They seem half-asleep, even when they're busy doing things they think are important. This is because they're chasing the wrong things. The way you get meaning into your life is to devote yourself to loving others, devote yourself to your community around you, and devote yourself to creating something that gives you purpose and meaning."

On Aging

"Aging is not just decay. . . . It's growth."

"If you're always battling against getting older, you're always going to be unhappy, because it will happen anyhow."

"You have to find what's good and true and beautiful in your life as it is now. Looking back makes you competitive. And, age is not a competitive issue."

chapter 8

Put Your Passions Out There
New beginnings are subtle and take much patience and persistence.

I wanted a perfect ending. Now I've learned, the hard way, that some poems don't rhyme and some stories don't have a clear beginning, middle and end. Life is about not knowing, having to change, taking the moment and making the best of it, without knowing what's going to happen next. Delicious ambiguity.
— *Gilda Radner*

New beginnings sometimes are subtle and take patience and persistence. There will always be reasons not to make the next move; sound reasons that everyone else — your spouse, your kids, your mother, and your local barista — will be happy to point out to you, if they haven't already occurred to you

Sometimes, you just have to smile, ignore them, and know that the power to transform your life is much closer than anyone — especially you — realizes. It *is* inside you. Start small. Appreciate small gains. Make gentle progress and keep putting your dreams out there.

The individuals in this chapter present some surprising and profound lessons about following your own calling and not doing what others think you should be doing.

Back to the Future

He fled the bright lights to find his soul and a simpler life-style.

> *We shall not cease from exploration. And the end of all our exploring will be to arrive where we started and know the place for the first time.*
> — *T. S. Eliot*

Jonathan Dokuchitz fled the limelight to pursue a simpler, quieter way of living. In moving ahead, he turned back to the future and a life he never imagined possible.

Jonathan Dokuchitz, 41, Gilbertsville, New York

Act I: Actor/singer in theater, film, and TV in New York City.

Act II: Business owner, Custom Electronics, Inc.

New Script

"To find a more peaceful balance of work/living/creativity after living as an employed actor in New York City for the past twenty-four years," says Jonathan. "It came about out of an inability to silence the voice in my soul telling me that it was time to find some quiet place to exist."

Life before the Leap

Jonathan had been acting since he was seventeen, in high school in Oneonta, New York. From the Cabaret Corps at the Williamstown Theatre Festival in the 1980s, to the La Jolla Playhouse in California, to Broadway theaters to the big screen, he created personas — Captain Walker in *The Who's Tommy* (nominated for fifteen Tony Awards) to Danny in *Sex in the City*, to *Two Weeks Notice,* and the past three and a half years as Corny Collins in *Hairspray.*

A self-described "very shy kid," Jonathan changed grade schools four times, and he spent his after-school and summer school vacations holed up in a car in the garage blasting tunes and singing along to his dad's Beach Boys, Beatles, and Carpenters eight-tracks. Karen Carpenter taught him to sing. "In high school, I managed to build up enough courage to audition for one of the musicals," he says. "When I finally made the cut, I realized that I was beyond comfortable on the stage. Standing in front of many was easier than to face a few." His sister, Diane, his mentor, traveled from Boston to see his debut high school performance in *Forum*. She told him early on, "Yes, I think you have it." Throughout the years, she would become his biggest fan, risking snowstorms at a moment's notice to see him as *Jack in the Beanstalk,* wearing a red wig and pulling a plaster cow on Broadway.

Even though Jonathan found himself on the professional stage in high school and was offered bigger and better roles, the then-teen assumed his destiny was to join his dad and older brothers in the electronics business his father founded forty-five years ago. Jonathan applied to a bunch of business schools. But Dad knew better, and he pushed his son to follow his passions and move to New York City to study acting.

There, Jonathan spent the next twenty-four years. The lure of the stage was intoxicating.

The Epiphany of Change

"But then the alarm clock rang," he says. "It was like the slow process of becoming conscious again. It was a new morning to face; my practical side was winning out after a long hibernation."

He discovered that he longed to reconnect with his family and simpler days. "I felt that I wanted something more. So mine is not so much a pursuit of fulfilling a lifelong dream, but that of finding a soft landing after the longest, most wonderful balloon ride."

In October 2007, with his dad turning eighty, Jonathan was pulled to step in and help run the family business; it seemed to be "the perfect getaway." "I realized after awhile that, although my experience on the stage would not in any way be helpful in designing an electronic capacitor, my experience with people and being creative was an asset that could be applied to any business."

But there was a lot of soul-searching to be done. "Was the need to help the family business just a convenient truth?" he remembers asking himself. "It seemed easier than baking cupcakes and selling real estate. It was an already established entity that wouldn't require me going to culinary school or 'actors in transition' workshop."

Standing on the Edge

There was no easy answer. "The day I sat in the president's office (of the electronics firm) telling him, 'Yes, I want to start working, basically full-time, starting October 1,' I felt the blood draining to my feet and a sick feeling of signing a deal with a devil or borrowing money from a bookie, knowing deep down, it isn't going to be pretty in the end."

"What pushed me off the cliff was the realization that we are not imprisoned with our choices," he states. "Unless we choose to be."

"As soon as I realized I could walk away at any time and resume my life in theater, the stones of worry and insecurity fell off me," he says. "I realized that if I just show up with a positive attitude, with no judgment about myself or the people around me, the steam engine would start to chug. And chug it did."

The Liftoff

His partner, Michael, also an actor, didn't speak to him for two weeks. Michael kept telling Jonathan, "You're an actor! You know nothing about capacitors!" Almost true.

But, another dream tugging at Jonathan was to live in an early 1800s house like the one from his childhood. "I grew up in a house that was circa 1805, a house I loved." The duo bought a 4,500-square-foot, 1857 Greek Revival house in a historic town of fewer than three hundred people and spent three years restoring it themselves, commuting back and forth to their apartment in the city.

"Talk about juxtapose," says Jonathan. "We were both practically in tears when we walked through it. It was a rainy day, and still light poured in through the floor-to-ceiling original lead glass windows"

Recapturing Lost Dreams

"That house went away along with my parents divorce, and I was heartbroken as a kid to see it go," he recalls. "I never dreamed that I might one day have a white elephant of my own to care for. Our rent-stabilized apartment in New York seemed like the good life, and then when we started to make some money and still couldn't afford to buy an apartment, I wasn't prepared to miss the boat."

The View from the Other Side

Walking away from New York City and relanding has been scary. But, the house itself evoked this in Jonathan: "It's the first time I've felt at home since I was nine. I feel like a rooted tree now, so it's hard for me to want to get on the road again. I've got a home that I can fill with friends, art, music, animals, and good food."

He's adjusting to the 9-to-5 shirt and tie. "I grew up with the business. I painted fences as a kid and sometimes answered the phones on summer vacation. I was duly qualified," says Jonathan. "I started slowly, very slowly. Getting up at 6 a.m.! I've slept till 11 a.m. for the past twenty-five years! Thank God for our dog, Bucky. His enthusiasm at that early hour, running through the woods, made me believe I could get used to this new life as well.

"The most rewarding thing for me is that, after feeling like an adolescent for all these years, I feel that I've made a firm commitment to myself as an adult," says Jonathan. "Not that I want to retire and play bridge, but the fact that I feel more responsible for myself and those around me after a life of not knowing where my next job was coming from is an empowering feeling."

These days, he still sometimes ventures into the city — and hops onto the stage. One gig he won't give up is singing at the jazz club Birdland, where he reunites with former friends from his Cabaret Corps days, when he used to sing with close friend Dana Reeve.

The occasional revisits help him stay focused on his new path and remember the journey and special moments of his first act. One of the most special was his close friendship with Dana.

"Dana's laugh and smile were magical," remembers Jonathan. "Hearing Dana's belly laugh was a treat to the senses. Like a warm breeze through the alto pipes of a wind chime. That was one of the best times of my life. Singing nonstop and meeting lifelong friends."

His ventures back remind him of how happy he is in his second act, too.

"I'm pleased when I go back to the city and see my friends doing all sorts of wonderful things," says Jonathan. "Being

Tips for Making the Jump

- *Create a "trust" plan.* "I'm finding it takes a lot of trust, patience, and a kick-ass calling plan."
- Stretch yourself. "Sudoku was running rampant in the theater dressing room, perhaps as if to ward off the inevitable Jell-O mold your brain has a tendency to turn into after doing the same thing for four years. I'd rather solve a real problem than a puzzle."
- *Take one day at a time.* "It's the first time, as far as I can remember, that I have had linear time to track and not some scattered Richter scale existence."
- *Maximize your impact.* "The most profound effect is on my dad. He never asked anything from me. He did, however, give me anything I asked for so that I could realize my dream. Now maybe he's helping me with my second act by allowing me to carry on his dream."

in the hot new show and working with the greats used to be everything to me. I feel the difference now, and it is telling. I don't wish it were me. I tell friends what I'm doing and, to my great surprise, they are excited for me and only support-ive. There is also a faraway glint in their eyes of wondering what that would be like. I see them imagine it for just a brief second, and for me, that moment of recognition of something other than performing is enough for me to feel okay.

"Michael [his partner] is adjusting nicely. My neighbors up here think I've gone nuts. Mostly, our dog, Bucky, is the hap-piest of us all. Running in the woods, rabbits to chase, and the occasional deer pellet to nibble on. It's heaven," says Jonathan.

Words to Inspire
"Part of the luxury of being an adult is to indulge yourself not in the recapturing, but the rearranging," says Jonathan.

Writing the Next Chapter
She taught the children well, then followed her heart and her pen to a new career.

The world breaks everyone, and afterward, many are strong at the broken places.
— Ernest Hemingway

"When you do the spiritual work to heal your bro-ken heart, your heart isn't just mended, it's new,

different, fresh, whole, healthy, and even holy," says
Janet Conner. She knows, the hard way.

Janet Conner, 60, Palm Harbor, Florida

Act I: Special education teacher; mother of son, Jerry
Koch, 16, a freshman at the New School in New
York City.

Act II: Spiritual writer, columnist, and teacher at *www.spiritualgeography.com* and *www.writingdownyoursoul.com*.

Life before the Leap

Janet did not set out to be a spiritual writer. A writing career
was nowhere on her radar screen. She has degrees in speech
pathology and education of the deaf, and she spent the first
ten years of her career teaching and administering educational programs for deaf children.

Side Tracks Along the Way

In the 1980s, she was offered a job at *CNN Headline News*
as an operations supervisor. "This turned out to be a blessing," she says. "Because this job wasn't about operations; it
was about hiring great people and keeping them focused and
happy — something a special ed administrator knows how to
do. And so, I fell into a career-changing job, and I ended up
creating the first video journalist hiring program at CNN."

That experience was enough to convince the founder of a
fledgling search firm that Janet could be a professional headhunter. After eleven years of recruiting, she opened a consulting practice to teach companies how to hire for themselves.

But with her fiftieth birthday approaching, Janet thought she had written the last chapter of her life experience. "I figured I'd earn a good living, give a few speeches every year, and basically live happily ever after," she says. "But you know that old joke: 'Want to see God laugh? Tell God your plans.' I can well imagine the Creator of the universe doubling over in stitches, as I proclaimed that my life was done."

Worst Moments

The more successful her business became, the more miserable her marriage. "In 1997, just as I was enjoying the first fruits of my new consulting practice, my marriage came to a screeching halt," she recalls. "When I told my husband I wanted a divorce — twenty-one years of trying was quite enough — he imploded, and my life disintegrated into wearing a police call necklace, keeping 911 predialed on my cell phone, and, on four occasions, taking my seven-year-old son into hiding. This disappearing act may have kept us safe from a drive-by shooting, but it also kept me cloistered away from clients. In response, they disappeared, along with most of my friends, and I found myself sitting in my living room with the blinds shut, sobbing on the sofa."

The Epiphany of Change

Then, providence stepped in.

"After two months of watching me cry, my Great Dane puppy pulled my untouched copy of *The Artist's Way* off the bookshelf, dragged it down the hallway, and plopped it on my lap," she remembers. "I got the message and started journaling right then and there. The book said to write three pages; I wrote thirty. The next day, and every day thereafter, I poured my heart and soul onto paper. I told God every ghastly detail of every ghastly thing that was happening and demanded — demanded! — help."

The Liftoff

The most amazing thing happened, she says. Help came. "It came in the form of questions I hadn't been willing to ask myself, ideas I needed to wrestle with, and little nuggets of wisdom I was long overdue to digest," she says. Suddenly, by writing my feelings, everything became more and more clear — the direction appeared."

The View from the Other Side

People noticed that talking to God every day in her journal transformed her life, and she began receiving offers to write for a local church and speak to their divorce recovery group. Her spiritual writing career was born.

"Three years later, my son and I were safe, my business was restored to twice its previous earnings, and I was able to buy a new townhome," she says. Things were looking good."

Words to Inspire

"My dream evolved, or rather I should say it hit me over the head, knocked me out, and when I came to, picked me up, dusted me off, turned me around, and shoved me in a new direction," says Janet. "I stumbled forward — there was no other option — but for several years, I kept looking back with wide eyes and empty pockets, calling out, 'Are you sure this is the right way?' And my angel — or whatever you want to call that deep messenger of the soul — kept smiling beatifically and pointing toward the vast black hole of the frightening unknown."

Making a Difference Every Day

For most of our lives, we have accepted our destinies. Now, we are choosing our own. In order to do so, it is necessary to take risks, to feel fear, and to make a commitment to our dreams. The best way to do so is to put them out there. No one knows what will happen when we change direction. But we have to go forward. We have to have faith, and we have to have the courage to seize every opportunity that is presented.

Here are five tips to help you move through the uncertainty to put your passions out there:

1. **Tap into your networks.** You want to get the word out that you are launching a new venture or at least that you are interested in exploring new opportunities. Send an e-mail to trusted friends, family, and those in your professional network, asking for their help to connect with others who may move your agenda.
2. **Check out professional organizations.** Are there associations, organizations, or clubs you could tap into to spread the word that you are venturing into this new field?

3. **Become an apprentice or volunteer:** The best way to test-drive your new path is to dive in and get a sampling of what it is like to actually run a foundation, start a small restaurant, or switch to a teaching career.

4. **Market yourself.** So you want to be a swimming coach? Post a flyer on the bulletin board of your local YMCA. There are also myriad Web sites, such as *www.craigslist.org*, where you can post your talent and professional services — or find opportunities to volunteer or sign up for an internship, and see if anyone is interested.

5. **Ask: "How will what I want to do make a difference in the world?"** When we are reinventing ourselves for a noble cause, good things are sure to come. How will the change in you, or surfacing the parts of you that make you unique, make the world a better place for others?

chapter 9

Become a Little Engine that Could
Develop that "I think I can" attitude.

*Nobody is born with courage. You have to develop
courage the same way you do a muscle.*
— Maya Angelou

Being a second act reinventor can take you out of a quiet
life of desperation and shine the spotlight on you, with lots
of people watching from the sidelines to see where you are
headed. The good news is that by the time you've arrived
at midlife you've probably developed a thicker skin. What
people think about you — and say publicly — doesn't matter
quite as much as it did when you were in your twenties.

Good, because the cries of naysayers will ring loudly.
Your best bet is to admit your fear, invest your energy in
moving forward (and not defending or deflecting their negative comments), and prepare for what lies ahead.

In this chapter, we focus on individuals who have located the inner strength to shake off criticism and the advice of well-meant but cautious others. A second act reinventor's mantra is, "I think I can, I think I can," even when they are climbing up the side of a steep mountain. What differentiates second act reinventors from those who sit out their second act is that the reinventors always stay focused on the view from top of the mountain and the essential question: *Whose life is it anyway?*

From Public Relations Guru to Photographer
The upshot of letting go was capturing "the most successful chapter of my career."

Whatever you can do, or dream you can, begin it. Boldness has genius, power and magic in it.
— Johann Wolfgang von Goethe

Karyn Millet was a highly successful PR guru and globe-trotter, but something meaningful was missing from her life. Today she captures hearts and souls with her camera lens.

Karyn R. Millet, 42, Santa Monica, California
Act I: Publishing and public relations executive.
Act II: Photographer.

New Script

Karyn worked in the fast-paced world of public relations, getting her clients in front of the camera. But she dreamed about getting behind the camera herself. She made a plan and set a goal: "To become a magazine photographer. It found me and happened very naturally."

Life before the Leap

As a Los Angeles public relations guru, Karyn stood behind the camera crew for fourteen years, staging, styling, and orchestrating photo shoots for clients. Much of her time was spent jet-setting the globe from Jamaica to Ireland, hustling luxury hotel properties.

The Epiphany of Change

Not a bad gig for most. But one day Karyn says, "I just hit the wall. I had to get out of what I was doing — fast."

"I finally decided it was time to get behind the camera and capture the image I always wanted," says Karyn. She quit with no idea what to do next and headed to her father's birthplace — Guatemala. Her father had died, and Karyn decided to use his ending to launch a new beginning for herself. There, she picked up a camera and learned Spanish. A month later, she came back to the sand and surf of her childhood, California, and enrolled in photography classes, became familiar with the camera, and launched her new career. She began selling photos she had taken in Guatemala. The vibrant colors, elaborate design motifs, and engaging architecture of the country's villages helped her focus on subject matter that continues to play a reoccurring theme in the images she captures.

"If something wants to be photographed, I shoot it," says Karyn. Having an academic background in interior design and decorative arts prior to her PR career, Karyn reached back to combine her design talent with her new dream. "While fellow photo students were focusing on trendy fashion shoots along train tracks, I was shooting living rooms and loving it," says Karyn.

Karyn took five lessons, and started saying "yes" to opportunities presented to her rather than waiting until she completed all the photography courses. "I sort of shot from the hip and learned as I worked," she says. "I happily immersed myself in photography."

The Liftoff

Without purposefully knowing so, Karyn followed the promptings of the early 1900s philosopher William James: "Act as if what you do makes a difference. It does."

Early on, she put together a solo show at a Los Angeles art gallery, which turned into a smashing debut performance: 150 people attended. She created and mailed out note cards with her photography, put up a Web site, and created promotional materials. "Most important, I followed up on every opportunity presented to me to maximize exposure. Rather than sit and ponder options, I dove headfirst into the deep end and tried to not look back."

Quickly her subject matter expanded to destinations near and far. From California beaches to Central America and

Europe, suddenly Karyn Millet photographs were popping up on the pages of home, garden, and travel & lifestyle magazines. "I think the secret was not overthinking things and just striving to do the best I could at each task each day. The next thing I knew, I had a national magazine cover," she says.

Inspired by Mentors

Karyn was inspired by two photographers she had hired frequently when she was in public relations. They were eager to help her, believed in her, and mentored her entry into the photography industry. They continue to be a source of encouragement. "I admire them a great deal. Honestly, it was others believing in me and giving me the confidence to forge ahead. This is something to remember and pass along to others when you see them about to hit their stride."

Another motivator is getting great pictures from each shoot. "To be able to capture a moment, to hold it and share it with others, is such a joy," says Karyn. "Also, having two magazine covers and one book cover last year (my second year shooting professionally) was beyond my wildest dreams."

For Karyn, her transformation and ability to let go and pursue her passion for photography is propelled by her faith. Each day she prayed, and continues to pray, "Let me decrease as you increase," meaning that she wanted to push her own will aside to let God's will take over. "When you realize you have the power of the Almighty behind you, it gives you the confidence to go beyond what you thought you were capable of."

The View from the Other Side

Today her clients include *O at Home, California Homes, Sunset, Traditional Home,* and more.

"I have been able to assemble a team and together we have conquered some pretty big shoots, and the camaraderie is contagious," she says. "Because of me taking big steps, it's helped others financially and professionally too, and that is very satisfying. I strive to help others in the same way my mentors were generous with their time and talents for me.

"I don't push a shot, but rather constantly have an eye out for the right light on an intriguing, poignant or subtle subject. With all the beauty that God gives each day, it is a welcome challenge to create a photograph that can hold the moment," she adds.

"I have been enjoying the most successful chapter in my career doing something I love," she says. "It can happen!"

Words to Inspire

"Lean on and trust in God. I encourage people to act upon the voices of those around you who encourage you, and keep taking steps forward each and every day," says Karyn.

Going Long

Two endurance athletes champion a buddy who lost his life to ALS in the summer of 2007.

> *Be the change you want to see in the world.*
> — *Mohandas Gandhi*

Often in life, it is the ability to pause and note those special moments in the blur of life that change us forever. Here, two jocks and training buddies were stopped in their tracks by the plight of another athlete, a guy who in the prime of his life had met his biggest opponent: ALS. They jumped in with all their grit and determination to help a guy who was once a stranger and now a friend. In doing so, they spawned a movement in the triathlete community that continues to spread like wildfire.

Meet John Wolski and Bob Mitera — change agents who said someone has to do something, and they did. They rallied to get thousands of others motivated and inspired to do something good within their athletic communities and way beyond.

John Wolski, 42, and Bob Mitera, 39
Palatine, Illinois, and Port Barrington, Illinois
   Act I: Senior Environmental Scientist; Project leader for Allstate Insurance Company; In the process of getting his MBA at Notre Dame.
   Act II: ALS activists and fund-raisers.

New Script
It's a story that began on the menacing lava fields of Kona, Hawaii, and recently played out for the third straight year in the sweaty corridors of the Buehler YMCA in Palatine, Illinois.

The heroes are three guys: John Wolski and Bob Mitera —
buddies who train together for Ironman races — and Jon
Blais, 35, a fellow endurance athlete from San Diego. Blais
"Blazeman" had won the hearts of millions in 2005 when he
became the first patient with Lou Gehrig's disease to literally
roll across the finish line of the Ironman Triathlon World
Championship in Hawaii.

Life before the Leap

John and Bob know all about battling cold, choppy waters,
pounding the pavement, and beating howling headwinds
to separate themselves from the pack. It's brutal. Both were
avid cyclists, runners, and swimmers, who got hooked on
the challenge of triathlons, especially the thrill of the ultimate triathlon — the Ironman.

In October 2005, Jon, who later earned the title "The
ALS Warrior Poet," completed the grueling Ironman course
in Kona, Hawaii, in 16 hours and 28 minutes.

The Epiphany of Change

They collectively challenged the merciless killer ALS, when
"Blazeman" lost his battle with ALS and died at age thirty-
five.

In the last several years of his life, despite his diagnosis,
Jon continued to train. A year before his death, he crossed
the finish line of the Kona Ironman.

His battle through the lava fields of Hawaii fresh in his
mind, and no longer able to compete himself, Blazeman

began assembling an army of multisport athletes for the War on ALS, organized to help end this disease. Those athletes, known as Team Blazeman Warriors, compete in multisport events around the world to raise awareness of ALS and valuable funds for research. The proceeds go to organizations dedicated to wiping out ALS and to individuals with ALS who are in need of financial assistance.

John and Bob are two of those warriors. Bob was in Kona coaching and working as a volunteer at the 2005 Ironman and was inspired after seeing Jon Blais cross the finish line and meeting Jon and his parents, Maryann and Bob.

Standing on the Edge

Blais's courage and indomitable spirit celebrate the triathletes' desire to win, but it also ignited a different breed of competitor in John and Bob. Bob says, "When I returned from Kona, my friend John and I were talking on a training run and the entire effort started to develop from there. When I found out that there is no cure for ALS, that the prognosis is the same as it was for Lou Gehrig — death — that just was unacceptable," says Bob. "We just said we have to do something to help this guy."

John adds, "He could have been any one of us. If your community doesn't help you, who will?"

What unfolds next is a story of endurance athletes across the globe rallying to make a difference in and on behalf of the lives of the nearly 20 million people who have died from ALS in the past twenty years.

The Liftoff

John and Bob set up their first event with a small group in the lobby of the Buehler YMCA in Palatine. The first year, 2006, there were four cyclists spinning for 16.5 hours. In 2007, dozens of cyclists kept fifteen bikes spinning for 10 straight hours. Year three, on February 9, 2008, nearly two hundred people kept all twenty bikes spinning for a total of 10 hours, raising more than $5,000 to support an ALS cure. A similar global event took place on March 1, 2008, as others from seventeen sites around the world gathered in health clubs, shopping malls, sporting goods stores, and home gyms.

The View from the Other Side

Today, what John and Bob started in 2005 by gathering a few training buddies has grown into a national event. Jon Blais flew out to meet his champions and friends in Illinois the first year the event was held. Last year, support rolled in from 17 sites nationwide.

Bob adds, "As Jon Blais said, the best part about this is we aren't Lance Armstrong with Nike behind us. We are just three hacks. Three regular guys and look what we've started."

Words to Inspire

"My dream is ongoing — it is to make each day the best it can possibly be for as many people as possible," says John. "I have always been someone who wants to see change where it is needed. Obviously, with no cure or treatment for ALS whatsoever, the need for action was obvious. And I've always been inspired by people who go beyond their comfort zone to be passionate about living life. It is rarer these days for people to really follow their passion — it seems as if people think there are just too many hurdles to overcome. I have to. That is the way I am wired. I cannot simply do nothing when there is a need in the community."

Making a Difference Every Day

We're not born with courage, and by midlife, if we haven't developed it as a mainstay, it's a constant test to muster the courage not to be disappointed with what we encounter when we risk stepping out of the comfortable.

So, how do we develop an "I think I can" attitude? How do we fight to the end to give birth to our newly reinvented

Tips from John Wolski and Bob Mitera

- Start small. Fix something up.
- Look around your school or your community and reach out to help someone who needs a little of your love.
- Pick your project and figure out what you need to make it work.
- Enlist friends for help.
- Spread your enthusiasm and help others see that you see a lot of potential just waiting to be discovered.

selves? We have to be committed. We have to stay on course and never give up. Here are tips on doing just that:

1. **Hang on tightly to enthusiasm.** Believing in what we want to do and why it is important in the world makes it happen.
2. **Dodge the blows.** Setbacks, unexpected events, and other interruptions often occur when we are in pursuit of our dreams. Cope with the difficulties, rest, reenergize, and jump back into the battle.
3. **Go beyond your limits.** Stretch yourself. Act as if your new life has begun in order to convince yourself that it is possible.
4. **Be committed.** Find ways to keep reaffirming your commitment.
5. **Let go and trust the mystery and the magic.** As author Paulo Coelho says, "God always offers us a second chance in life."

chapter 10

Stay Focused
You can make it to the finish line.

Ever tried. Ever failed. No Matter.
Try again. Fail again. Fail better.
— *Samuel Beckett*

True change takes commitment and practice, practice, practice. It's hard to take the many, many numerous small steps needed to make the one big one. In this chapter, we look at how second act reinventors ease into change and have the patience to believe it really will come, even if it means waiting, and practicing, for years.

Their advice: You have to learn to break your reinvention into bite-sized pieces. Then, it will come. And you have to keep trying, sometimes again and again. These second act reinventors all agree: "If at first you don't succeed, try again."

Rocky Mountain High

This futures trader climbs every mountain forging a life that feeds his heart and soul.

To strive, to seek, to find, and not to yield.
— Ulysses

David Reiner was an accomplished futures trader with his own seat on the Chicago Board of Trade when he started feeling pangs of wanderlust. Then, he fell madly in love — with the mountains. He now has a whole new view on life. He held on to the following quote from Howard Thurman, author, to make his dreams come true:

> Don't ask yourself what the world needs. Ask yourself what makes you come alive and go do that, because what the world needs is people who have come alive.

David Reiner, 51, Highland Park, Illinois (April through September); Crested Butte, Colorado (October through March)

Act I: CPA, accounting firm.

Act II: Trader, Chicago Board of Trade.

Act III: Volunteer and seeker.

Act IV: Yoga teacher, guest services ambassador, and volunteer ski instructor for the disabled.

New Script

It was a vision he'd harbored for more than twenty years that lured David to the charming, historic Rocky Mountain ski resort town of Crested Butte, Colorado, more than 1,000 miles from his home in Chicago's North Shore of Highland Park.

Ever since he had taken a summer vacation to Colorado when he was in his thirties, David dreamed of living in a beautiful mountain town. "I wanted to be able to pursue my passions of the outdoors," says David. "I love the majesty of mountains and feel uplifted spiritually in their presence. My first experience in the mountains struck a deep chord inside and a desire to make living a mountain life manifest. I had never hiked in the mountains before. From that point on, my heart was connected to this incredible beauty."

Life before the Leap

David would live in the place many people can relate to, looking at his dream from afar. As a husband and father of three young children, David began his career as a CPA for a large accounting firm. Number crunching and the corporate scene were not his thing. He was just about to flee for southern California and the pursuit of an MBA when he met the woman who would become his wife and decided to plant roots and stay in Chicago.

That's when an opportunity to buy in as a floor trader presented itself. Fueled by the need to make real money for his young family, David found he was pretty good at the trader gig and became an almost overnight success, making a lot of money from the get-go.

"I loved trading and was very successful," he says. "I felt it was the ultimate opportunity to allow my own skills to directly affect my success. I thrived on the competition and the challenge. Also, being my own boss was right for my personality. Each day was a different opportunity to utilize my talents as a trader."

The Epiphany of Change

Over the years the markets changed, and David began feeling less and less of a pull to do what he was doing. "The trading became more tedious and difficult," he recalls. "Since I had built financial support over the years, I lost my drive and motivation to succeed. It became more of a place to be rather than a love for what I was doing."

Standing on the Edge

He says he felt a desperation to get out and so he did, fast. In 1988, he left the trading pits to pursue life as a full-time volunteer. He had saved a substantial amount of money from his trading days, and so he says he was lucky to have the option not to work and pursue his passions. And so he poured his energy into giving to others — visiting kids at Children's Memorial Hospital and bringing his dog, Spunky, to visit patients at hospitals throughout the Chicago area.

David began studying yoga and Pilates. "The idea of mind/body exercise was very interesting," he recalls. He became certified to teach Pilates and taught for two years in a studio close to his Highland Park home. But he began losing interest in "just teaching exercise" and was drawn to the more spiritual practice of yoga. "I left the studio and stopped teaching altogether," he recalls.

"I was not happy about being in Highland Park and really wanted to start a new life in the mountains," he says. "I struggled with this personal conflict since my wife would not move away and I did not want to be a part-time dad. I stayed in Chicago to raise my kids. This was very difficult since I felt strongly about not wanting to have a life in the Chicago suburbs. Financially I was set and nothing kept me. But I was too strongly against leaving my family and pursuing life on my own out West."

The Liftoff

In September 2003, David was diagnosed with non-Hodgkin's lymphoma, a fast-growing cancer. He views it as a gift.

"This experience helped me in so many ways," says David. "I was able to give up old patterns. I credit some of this to the cancer. My body was so weak that things I held on to on a physical level, I could no longer hold on to them. I was able to give up old patterns that kept me back from truly connecting and enjoying life. Going through this experience, I was able to shift and realized that if I had the chance I would live differently."

With his cancer in remission, David began teaching yoga classes and pursued formal training under the tutelage of John Friend, founder of Anusara yoga. The philosophy of Anusara yoga is centered in a celebration of the heart and looks for the good in all people and things.

Tapping into his heart and inspired to pursue his dream again, David tried to make mountain living a reality in

1990, renting a home in Park City, Utah, with his family for the summer. But, his wife, Lynn Reiner, the president of a women's art association and an art teacher, was eager to return to their Highland Park home. His children — Jennifer, Jonathan, and Jacqueline — all in their teens and early twenties — wanted to be in suburban Chicago as well.

But David kept having vivid dreams about the mountains and a stirring restlessness in his soul. David paid attention to the restlessness.

"Someday I knew that my dream would be fulfilled," he says. "My personal growth was helped by an extremely gifted, loving therapist," says David. "Doing deep, difficult heart work with him allowed for shift, growth, and transformation to occur.

"I was at a crossroads in my family, professional, and emotional life. I needed help sorting out all these issues. I felt inside things were not right. I was unhappy. I did the hard personal growth work to transform and change. Things in my life took a new positive direction, and everything seemed to come together when I got sick," he adds.

Finally, with two of his children graduated from college and a third a university student in Denver, David and his wife made a deal to live half the year in Crested Butte, Colorado, making their move in October 2007. "I am living my dream each day," he enthuses.

The View from the Other Side

"This small, friendly community feels just right," he says. "Each day I walk outside, there is a feeling of uplift as I gaze out to the sky. My eyes are filled with incredible beauty and my heart is right at home."

There, he teaches Anusara yoga classes at a studio in town, which pumps up his energy level and enthusiasm daily. He and his wife also work at a ski resort in guest services once a week and ski. David volunteers for an adaptive sports program teaching children with disabilities how to ski.

"It is truly inspiring to be part of their joy," he says. "Life here has given me a sense of complete freedom. I truly love the feeling of being in the mountains. I feel now that my kids are out of high school, I no longer have to be in Highland Park. I finished what I needed to do there as a dad. I am now able to pursue fully what I want. This feels great.

"I pass these positive feelings on in all my relationships, and as a teacher, I am inspired to live life completely and fully and try to encourage others to view their own passions and follow as best they can," says David.

"My intention is to live fully in the now — positively and deeply in my heart," says David. "People need to ask themselves what is it they want. What do they have to give up in order to get what they want and what action do they need to take?

"I wanted to live life out in the mountains, but I would have had to give up being a dad and having full involvement and connection with my children. This did not work for me. I needed to be a father to my children more than having a life out West. I did not like my life in Chicago, but leaving there meant I could not be the father I needed to be to my children. Thus the dilemma that caused a lot of frustration.

I tried to give myself as much as I could with trips out West. Also, making my life more meaningful by teaching yoga in Chicago and trying to fill my time with things that were positive and fulfilling for me."

Words to Inspire

"If people are not living their dream life, I suggest they try to put the focus on what they can do in the meantime to give themselves hits of what it is they need," says David.

Going the Extra Mile

Inspired by his daughter's illness, this firefighter dad picks up his running shoes, dons a wet suit, and hops on his cycle to race for a cure for leukemia. He inspires the whole family to get into fund-raising, waging war on childhood cancers to help others win the race.

> You really can change the world if you care enough.
> — Marion Wright Edelman

Barb Horn would be the first to describe her family as just your average suburban American clan leading a "crazy" busy life juggling baseball, soccer, and three kids' busy activity schedule.

Then, cancer swooped in, turning their lives upside down. For three years, the family rallied alongside

Maggie, who was diagnosed with leukemia at age six. Today, she is a healthy sixth grader. And in mega pay-it-forward fashion, the Horns are still waving the banner and leading the pack on the war against childhood cancer year-round through their own grassroots efforts.

Barb Horn, 45, and Bill Horn, 46, Franklin Park, Illinois

Act I: Barb devoted her life to be "mom" to Ryan, Maggie, and Allie.

Bill: Franklin Park Fire Department lieutenant.

Act II: Following Maggie's cancer and remission, the family became crusaders in the battle against childhood cancer; Bill joined Team in Training for the Leukemia & Lymphoma Society; and later, the whole family became organizers of a local St. Baldrick's Foundation fund-raiser.

New Script

If anyone needs proof that our children inspire us as parents to "go the extra mile," Bill provides it. In 2007, Bill competed in a grueling adventure that involved a 1.2-mile swim, a 56-mile bike ride, and a 13-mile run. Crossing the finish line at the Steelhead Half-Ironman triathlon in Benton Harbor, Michigan, Bill had tears in his eyes and the vision of what was driving him in his heart.

Her name is Maggie.

And jumping up and down at the finish line and holding out her hand to run across it with him was the twelve-year-old dynamo herself, along with Bill's wife Barb, Maggie's little sister Allie and older brother Ryan cheering from the sidelines.

"You can do it, Dad!" screams Bill's #1 cheerleader — daughter Maggie. These days the sixth grader is a catcher on a travel softball team and an aspiring Iron "woman" herself. "When I'm eighteen, I'm doing it with my dad" she enthuses.

And then she smiles at him, and teases, "You'll be an old man then, Dad, like what, fifty-two? You better watch out for me." In addition to once sporting the same "do" (Bill shaved his hair to show Maggie he was in the fight with her 24/7 during her chemo), this dad-daughter duo share the same birthday: September 25.

No question. Maggie is unstoppable.

As the patient honoree for the Chicagoland Leukemia & Lymphoma Society's chapter of Team in Training, Maggie is the poster child of the indomitable human spirit. The national organization uses events such as the Steelhead Half-Ironman to raise millions of dollars to fund research and clinical trials.

Life before the Leap

Bill, a firefighter, and Barbara, a stay-at-home mom lived the "typical" suburban family life, ushering their three young children to soccer games and school activities, determined to raise strong, healthy children. That was before their middle child, Maggie, was diagnosed with cancer. Life for the Horn's changed dramatically. Today, they are committed to helping other families through the confusion and fear of childhood cancer.

The Epiphany of Change

Now in remission, Maggie was diagnosed with acute lymphocytic leukemia in December 2001, when she was in kindergarten. She endured two and a half years of countless blood draws, spinal taps, and bone marrow draws, as well as chemotherapy treatments.

Bill remembers the day Maggie was diagnosed. He was driving back from Children's Memorial Hospital in Chicago late at night to get home to Allie and Ryan, when the Beatles song "Here Comes the Sun" started playing.

"I was just crying," says Bill. "But I knew we were going to do everything we could to fight this for Maggie." During Maggie's illness, Bill, Barb, Allie, and Ryan made a pledge to Maggie: "We'll get you through this. We are a family, we are a team, and we are all in this together."

Standing on the Edge

Bill has been tirelessly committed to this challenge since the day he witnessed other Team in Training members competing on behalf of Maggie, who was named the patient honoree.

"I thought if all these people can do this on behalf of Maggie, I can too," says Bill, who was motivated to enter his first triathlon. And so, outside of Maggie's hospital room he began training hard, day and night, whenever a free moment became available.

Bill says the reason that he decided to test his athletic mettle is to raise money that goes toward research and patient care for those who have been diagnosed with a blood-related cancer. While the feats initially seemed daunting for a fireman who was in "okay" shape but had never trained for this swim/bike/run endurance sport, Bill knew they were nothing compared to what Maggie had endured.

"She never complained, even during the worst," says Barb. "She'd be like, 'Mom, don't worry, I am going to be okay.'"

It's a Family Affair

The Horns also have spent the past two years staging a unique grassroots campaign to champion critically ill kids through organizing a local dinner event for the international St. Baldrick's Foundation. They've orchestrated events of up to seven hundred people in 2007 and more than nine hundred in 2008, raising nearly $200,000 for the cause. And Maggie arms herself with scissors and the mantra "Bald can be beautiful" to shave her dad's head as thousands of others nationwide go bald to raise money for the cause. At the event, more than 200 men had their heads shaved to raise money for children's cancers. St. Baldrick's is a global fund-raising organization for children's cancer. In eight years, events have taken place in eighteen countries, raising $49.5 million, and shaving 71,000 heads.

"I told my dad, I would always help get him through it," says Maggie, referring to the triathlons. Same goes for the entire family, who cheer dad Bill on at the finish line and play a huge role in the planning and running of the St. Baldrick's fund-raiser.

The View from the Other Side

Indeed, after cancer entered their lives so dramatically, Barb and Bill Horn have found their lives more different than they ever imagined. Yes, they are the busy parents of active kids, but under the surface, their every hour, their second act, is framed in reaching out to other parents and families facing the unimaginable: their child's cancer.

"How could we do anything else," says Barb. "We feel we have to help.

"We're a success story, even though we've had some bumps in the road. It has been nothing compared to what some families go through," says Barb. "When Maggie got sick, we said, 'We are going to fight this as a family team together.' Now, we are a team that is going to help other families."

Now captain of the extended friends, family, and firehouse cheerleading squad, Maggie is the female Vince Lombardi of the Chicago-area Team in Training's triathlon group. During the pasta carb-loading parties staged on the eve of events, she stands at the podium in front of dozens of athletes and their friends and families and inspires them to personal record feats. And, she is the most popular girl at the dance at the St. Baldrick's gathering. The entire Horn family helps Bill train and cheers him at the finish line, and helps organize the St. Baldrick's event.

So whether it is competing in a triathlon for the leukemia charity or rallying folks to a party at a banquet hall, Bill and

Barb and their family are committed to living a second act —
with their kids playing leading roles — that is all about helping
others, just like the families that reached out to help them.

Words to Inspire

"This is what our future is going to be all about," says Barb.
"We took on Maggie's cancer as a family, and we're all in this
together, helping other families."

Making a Difference Every Day

Most reinventors confess to feeling impatient. People will say
that change takes years — and years are not something we
feel we have in abundance when we are eager to kick-start
our second acts. So how do we stay focused and dedicated to
our transformation?

Here are five tips to help us stay positive and productive
so that we can follow our hearts, jump on the roller coaster,
and ride out our dreams:

1. **Seek out like-minded people.** They will affirm and en-
   ergize you to stay focused and positive.
2. **Stay excited about the possibilities.** Let your imagina-
   tion wander.
3. **Ignore the negatives.** Don't let your fears zap your energy.
4. **Change what you can.** Try to let go of what you can't
   change.
5. **Set goals.** Announce them to others who will keep you
   on task and on target.

chapter 11

Make the Change You Want to See in the World

You've accomplished the feat that you set out to do. Now what?

*Whatever you receive, wherever it comes from,
cherish the desire to give it back in full measure.*
— *Swami Chidvilasananda*

Congratulations! You have spent months, if not years, and lots of energy trying to discern a "second act that makes a difference." You've decided what you really want, who you really are, and that it is time to make the change, to step out and put your passion into the universe.

Starting to make the changes you want to make in your life is a step-by-step process. In order to get started, create a plan for yourself that answers the following questions. When you can clearly articulate your "elevator speech," you are ready to reach out to the world to put your vision into reality. Your personal "elevator speech" is a one-paragraph description that succinctly describes what you want your life to be. Ask yourself: What does your new work mean to you and why? How do you want to help others? Identify what your motivations are. Identify what the pinnacle of success would be. Most importantly, remember it is a journey, not a destination. Now start moving toward what you want.

> Love yourself first and everything else falls into line. You really have to love yourself to get anything done in this world.
> — *Lucille Ball*

Legacy of Hope

From sales to social work to medical school, to lung cancer crusader, this mom follows the inexplicable to her dreams.

> *You have to celebrate the gifts because life is so hard and I think once you realize life's gonna be hard, the good stuff really comes forward.*
> — *Dana Reeve*

After her sister, Dana Reeve, died in March 2006, Deborah Morosini became a champion and crusader in the war against lung cancer. Today, she's a board member for the Bonnie J. Addario Lung Cancer Foundation, traveling the country to bring her message and champion a cure.

Deborah Morosini, M D , 49, Weston, Massachusetts

Act I: Regional sales manager for a textile firm in New York City; Master's degree in social work.

Act II: Medical school; research and development pathologist; wife to Charles and mother of sons James and Peter.

Act III: Champion and crusader in the war against lung cancer; board member for the Bonnie J. Addario Lung Cancer Foundation, traveling the country to bring her message and champion a cure.

Life before the Leap

Deborah will tell you that every day is a second act, that there are many second acts. She knows firsthand, because she's had about five of them.

All through her childhood and early careers, she had pursued all things "right brained," she acknowledges. She had a dream job as a social worker that went with her image of what life in New York City is supposed to be about. Then, she became a sales manager for an architectural fabric company — Gretchen Bellinger — in the Big Apple.

But that wasn't enough.

The tugging for Deborah was to "develop parts of myself that I had not used — the extremely logical and fact-based parts of my brain that were dormant."

She began medical school part-time at night, while she worked her full-time day job in sales. "I had no science background, so I had to start from the very beginning with very basic math," she says.

A little voice inside herself told her to keep going, despite the obstacles.

"I just ploughed through with a huge amount of determination," says Deborah.

"When I entered med school, I had a newborn, and I arranged to go to school part-time," says Deborah, who started medical school at age 30. "I had another son two years later, and after that I got divorced. So I had a two-year-old and a four-year-old and was a single mom in medical school. I did not really feel like I had much choice in the matter at that point."

In 2005, she was swimming in the success and the relative calm of her life as mom of James and Peter, wife to Charlie, and pathologist for AstraZeneca. She'd come a long way from the days of being a single mom in medical school with two preschoolers.

The Epiphany of Change

But then, in 2004, her brother-in-law Christopher Reeve died. The next year, her mom, Helen, died.

In August 2005, Deborah and her husband Charlie and two teenaged sons were at Logan International Airport in Boston, shuffling through security and biding time while waiting to embark on a family vacation to India.

Glancing up at the television monitors, Deborah and her family would be reminded, over and over and over again, of the crushing news the world was just learning: Dana Reeve, 44, wife of Superman Christopher Reeve, Deborah's little sister, and the boys' aunt, had been diagnosed with Stage 4 lung cancer.

"It all happened in such a public way," says Deborah. "Being stuck at an airport with the TV news repeating it over and over was just not a great place to be. It was devastating."

Standing on the Edge

Seven months later, Dana, tireless crusader for paralysis, mother extraordinaire for her son Will, and Mother of the Year for the American Cancer Society, would lose her battle with lung cancer. A nation, glued to their televisions again, would express their shock and mourn deeply the loss of Dana, whom they had come to embrace as the epitome of a woman filled with grace, courage, and determination.

"Life isn't supposed to happen the way it did for our family," says Deborah. "Chris had died. My mother had just died, and now Dana was diagnosed with lung cancer.

"I realized then that you become a survivor the moment you are diagnosed. You decide right now this is all happening, but my sister is still alive, yes she is really sick. But we need to live in the moment. She is still here and we need to put our worries aside."

The Liftoff

Certainly, Dana and Christopher Reeve had become public icons of survival and inspirations following the 1995 horse-back-riding accident that left Christopher a vent-dependent quadriplegic. Together, with their laserlike focus on paralysis and stem cell research, the couple and the forces they rallied shone a spotlight on an injury for which research was poorly funded. They made it a cause.

Now, for the second time, the world would focus its lens on a disease that for a long time had been swept under carpet as the "stigma cancer."

"From Chris we were inspired, okay, see what happened with this, now we might be able to make a shift in the way we look at lung cancer," says Deborah.

Today, in addition to her full-time job as pathologist and role as mom to two teens, Deborah serves on the board for the Bonnie J. Addario Lung Cancer Foundation, traveling the country to give talks on the urgency of finding a cure for lung cancer.

The View from the Other Side

"Dana and Christopher showed the world that despite illness, despite fate, despite forces we can't control, the only thing you can control is what you leave behind," says Deborah. "Now it is my turn to carry that on for them," she says. "It's no co-incidence that I trained for so many years to be a doctor and pathologist trying to break the mystery around cancer. I just didn't imagine I would be doing it on behalf of my sister."

In just a little more than a year, her crusade has led to un-forgettable lessons of hope, frustration, and how to navigate a maze of funding, government, and stigma roadblocks that cloud the issue and keep treatment and cures for this deadly cancer elusive. She's determined to raise public awareness of lung cancer to step up research and support for the cause.

So, when she's not at work researching cancer as a pathologist at AstraZeneca or taking care of her two teenaged sons, Deborah has made it her life's passion and mission to speak to audiences, legislators—anyone who will listen—about the terrible tragedy of her sister's death, the effects of lung cancer, and the lack of available treatment for it today.

Beyond fighting to raise awareness about lung cancer, Deborah says one of her most important roles is to carry her sister's indemonstrable spirit for living fully to the world. And she has no intention of fading away from whatever challenges lie ahead.

"I can't speak enough; I can't do enough, until we're taken seriously and the tragedy of lung cancer is over," says Deborah.

Deborah is ready to forge ahead.

Words to Inspire

"My sister and Chris created a positive legacy. They showed the world that out of crisis, you can make a life; you can have a sense of humor and not fall apart. They touched so many people . . . people including myself, who maybe looked at them and then said, 'Okay, I can get through this. . . . I can remain optimistic.'"

Creating a Bountiful Farmer's Market

Good-bye city life. Green acres here we come.

There are moments when you must be prepared to take a risk and do something crazy.
— *Paulo Coelho*

Don and Trese Larson left their comfy suburban digs to head to the country and start planting a new life for themselves — one that gives back to the world with abundance.

Don, 48, and Trese, 47, Larson, Roscoe, Illinois

Act I: Don: Retailing and several manufacturing jobs; Trese: Nurse practitioner.

Act II: Don: undergraduate degree in jazz studies and music instructor.

Act III: 2007: Owners of Pine Row Farm, a five-acre sustainable agriculture farm; co-founders of a community supported agriculture (CSA) cooperative. Trese continues her nursing position while also raising a herd of dairy goats and using their milk to create luxury soap.

New Script

Trese and Don are having a hen party of sorts. At their dream farm in Roscoe, Illinois, the duo manages a small flock of heritage breed laying hens and dairy goats raised on pasture and organic-based feed. The produce — heirloom toma-toes, Italian sweet peppers, root crops, salad and cooking greens, cultivated in their small market garden — is sold at local farmer's markets and mailed to customers through their Tomorrow's Harvest food cooperative.

As owners of Pine Row Farm (named for the acre of pines on the property), Trese and Don are part of a "com-munity supported agriculture" movement that has grown vigorously in recent years. "It's going back to the way it was a hundred years ago, where a family goes to the local farm to sustain themselves,'" says Don. "It's the community, going back to the land that people like."

Life before the Leap

Saxophonist Don always dreamed of catering to neighbors' tastes for fresh vegetables, homemade cheeses, and other farm novelties, like those grown on the farms surrounding his boyhood home in Rockford, Illinois.

For the first almost two decades of their marriage, Don worked a variety of jobs he describes as on the fringe of his agriculture aspirations — behind the machinery at a meat and cheese processing company, repairing farm buildings, and an assortment of retail jobs that he says paid the mort-gage, "but were never what I wanted in my heart."

Says Don: "When I was younger, we had family friends who worked a conventional farm and would often spend time there in the summer. I loved it."

But in 2001, Don says he started getting serious about "what I was going to do with the rest of my life." He and

Trese moved to Wisconsin so he could begin his undergraduate degree. "I came to college late in life," explains Don.

At first attending school in Wisconsin to get his degree in saxophone performance and jazz studies, Don transferred to DePaul University in Chicago to complete his degree, commuting an hour-and-a-half each way from the couple's Wisconsin home. "I spent a lot of long nights on the train wracking my brain thinking about what I want to do in life," says Don. Following graduation, he began teaching private music lessons.

But the drought in his heart kept nagging, and private music instruction wasn't as lucrative as he would have liked. "I loved music, but I always really wanted to be a farmer. And I wanted to find something that would allow Trese to retire and do what she loved too."

The Liftoff

Don's dream fell into his lap almost by accident. A realtor in his hometown of Rockford told him and Trese about a small ranch house on five acres that was up for sale in the neighboring town of Roscoe. "We wanted to move back to this area, but at first we thought that there was no way we could afford it," says Don. After a few strategic negotiations, the owners of the house accepted their offer, and Don and Trese decided that they would take a risk and try to make a living off the land.

"I knew I wanted to do more than just mow grass all summer," Don says. "Of course I was terrified, but knew if I didn't try, we would be letting our dream die."

As luck would have it, their five-acre homestead was originally part of a conventional farm for many years; sweet corn and hay were the primary crops. But the farmland was transformed into a subdivision in the 1970s, divided into five-acre plots.

The first years were born with trial and error.

"We bought a few books on market gardening, but had very little success," says Don.

Then the couple sought out learning opportunities and signed up for a program that teaches beginner farmers. They also signed up to volunteer working with a local farmer.

"Small-scale vegetable farming is the ultimate challenge," says Don. "We fight against weather conditions, small and large pests, livestock predators, equipment breakdown, personal health (my back wishes I was 24, not 48!), outrageous land prices, and worst of all, government regulations. Success comes not as often as we need it to, but when it does, it is truly worth celebrating."

The View from the Other Side

These days, Don and Trese are turning buying vegetables into somewhat of an event. They have joined forces with a group of four local formers to launch the Tomorrow's Harvest Cooperative. The group is unique among community-supported agriculture (CSA) outfits because it brings the very best of four individual farms to the table. Each farm grows something special, something best, and this food is packed up and shipped to members weekly. Customers are those who are drawn to the taste and quality of local food and increasingly want to know where their food is coming from. That's something to celebrate, as more and more consumers are going directly to small local farms to buy their produce, and many are becoming share members of such programs — an auspicious reflection of the growth of the organic food movement.

The couple's secret of success: "Timely weeding is money in the bank," laughs Don. He admits, though, that pursuing his dream has been challenging. When the Larson family was on an Alaskan cruise for Don's parents' wedding anniversary,

Starring Roles

Many celebrities are redefining midlife and celebrating second acts:

- Kevin Bacon
- Anita Baker
- Alec Baldwin
- Ellen DeGeneres
- Patricia Heaton
- Holly Hunter
- Madonna
- Megan Mullaly
- Michelle Pfeiffer
- Prince
- Sharon Stone

he had to stay home to tend the farm. He has a trailer full of four hundred tomato plants that he can't get in the ground because it's been too wet to plant them.

The rewards, however, outweigh the work. While eating an anniversary dinner with Trese at an elegant restaurant he does business with, Don spotted his own beets and carrots on customers' plates. "People are very appreciative of fresh produce, and I like being able to provide that. It's very rewarding to see someone enjoy something we grew," Don says.

Words to Inspire

"Forget the whole corporate mentality of 'guard your secrets.' If you are looking to follow your passion, find other people who are going after the same dream and don't be afraid to ask them for help. I have found that the mentors and friends I have made in farming would help me in a split second if I ever needed them for anything. People with dreams want others to succeed too."

Making a Difference Every Day

If you're reading this book, you're probably struggling to reinvent your second act into something significant because you want to make an impact on the world, to make a difference in the lives of others. You may have asked yourself how ordinary people can make extraordinary differences in the lives of others. You ask, *What is the meaning of my life?*

Here are five ideas that that will help you jump-start your determination to make a difference in the world:

1. **Start with yourself.** It is impossible to make a meaningful difference in someone else's life without making a meaningful difference in our own. So follow your dreams to reinvent.

2. **Be the change you want to see in the world.** You can't change the world all by yourself, but you can decide how you live your life. Live according to your ideals and what you believe in. Do what matters to you. You can't control how others live, but you can control your own life.

3. **Ask yourself who you can help.** Look around for the people who may need and want your help. Explore what you can do to make a positive influence in their lives.

4. **Volunteer.** Check out the organizations, groups, and events where you can make a difference by volunteering, donating your time or talent.

5. **Ask for guidance.** When you're ready to make a difference in the world, don't hesitate to reach out and seek help in finding the opportunities that exist for you. They are there; you just need to connect with them.

So Where Do You Go from Here?

What is it within you that says you have a second act coming? And a third? And a fourth? Life is about reinvention. We're never done, as long as we're still writing the book about ourselves and creating new chapters. So, the questions should never stop. Second act reinventors believe we should always heed the yearning to stretch beyond our wildest dreams.

When we do, we are not just helping ourselves but shining a beacon of hope for all to see.

If there is one lesson learned from the second act reinventors in this book, it is to follow your heart . . . always. And always remember, that when we embrace our own authentic lives, we can't help but bring something greater back into the world.

So go, chase your dreams. And know that in bringing your dreams to life, you are giving life and hope to everyone around you.

Books to Inspire and Guide You

Mitch Albom. *Tuesdays with Morrie*. Anchor Books, 1997.

Kate Braestrup. *Here If You Need Me: A True Story*. Little, Brown and Company, 2007.

Julia Cameron. *The Artist's Way*. Tarcher, 2002.

Nadine Condon. *Hot Hits, Cheap Demos: The Real-World Guide to Music Business Success*. Backbeat Books, 2003.

Joan Didion. *The Year of Magical Thinking*. Knopf, 2005.

Claudia Kawczynska. *Dog Is My Co-Pilot: Great Writers on the World's Oldest Friendship*. Three Rivers Press, 2003.

——— *Howl: A Collection of the Best Contemporary Dog Wit*. Crown, 2007.

Thomas Moore. *A Life at Work: The Joy of Discovering What You Were Born to Do*. Broadway, 2008.

Jeannie Morris. *Brian Piccolo: A Short Season*. Dell Publishing, 1972.

Parker Palmer. *Let Your Life Speak: Listening for the Voice of Vocation*. Josey Bass, 2000.

Gilda Radner. *It's Always Something*. Simon and Schuster, 1989.

Howard Thurman. *Meditations of the Heart*. Beacon Press, 1999.

Marianne Williamson. *The Age of Miracles: Embracing the Mid-Life*. Hay House, 2008.

About the Author

Mary Beth Sammons is an award-winning journalist and women's issues columnist. Her work appears frequently in *Family Circle*, the *Chicago Tribune*'s lifestyle section, and in leading consumer women's magazines. She is currently the "Finding You" editor for *www.BettyConfidential.com* and writes for various health and business publications. As a vice president of editorial, Mary Beth launched the editorial departments for the largest consumer health Web site — *RevolutionHealth.com* and its subsidiary, *CarePages.com*, for which she writes separate blogs. In addition, she is currently working with the Stanford Research Institute as editorial director of a storytelling project focused on consumer health and wellness. She specializes in stories that inspire ordinary people to do extraordinary things from a place deep in their hearts. She has written six books in the women's self-help and mind/body/health field, including *We Carry Each Other: Getting Through Life's Toughest Times*, Conari Press, 2007. She lives in Chicago's suburbs with her three children.

photo © Suzanne Plunkett, Chicago

To Our Readers

Conari Press, an imprint of Red Wheel/Weiser, publishes books on topics ranging from spirituality, personal growth, and relationships to women's issues, parenting, and social issues. Our mission is to publish quality books that will make a difference in people's lives — how we feel about ourselves and how we relate to one another. We value integrity, compassion, and receptivity, both in the books we publish and in the way we do business.

Our readers are our most important resource, and we value your input, suggestions, and ideas about what you would like to see published. Please feel free to contact us, to request our latest book catalog, or to be added to our mailing list.

Conari Press
An imprint of Red Wheel/Weiser, LLC
500 Third Street, Suite 230
San Francisco, CA 94107
www.redwheelweiser.com